THE **W** ORD ON

PRAYER
AND THE
Devotional Life

JIM BURNS
THE NATIONAL INSTITUTE OF YOUTH MINISTRY

Gospel Light

Gospel Light, is an evangelical Christian publisher dedicated to serving the local church. We believe God's vision for Gospel Light is to provide church leaders with biblical, user-friendly materials that will help them evangelize, disciple and minister to children, youth and families.

We hope this Gospel Light resource will help you discover biblical truth for your own life and help you minister to youth. God bless you in your work.

For a free catalog of resources from Gospel Light please contact your Christian supplier or call 1-800-4-GOSPEL.

PUBLISHING STAFF
Jean Daly, Editor
Kyle Duncan, Editorial Director
Gary S. Greig, Ph.D., Senior Editor
Mary Gross, Contributing Writer

ISBN 0-8307-1643-2
© 1994 Jim Burns
All rights reserved.
Printed in U.S.A.

How to Make Clean Copies from This Book

You may make copies of portions of this book with a clean conscience if:

• you (or someone in your organization) are the original purchaser;

• you are using the copies you make for a noncommercial purpose (such as teaching or promoting your ministry) within your church or organization;

• you follow the instructions provided in this book.

However, it is ILLEGAL for you to make copies if:

• you are using the material to promote, advertise or sell a product or service other than for ministry fundraising;

• you are using the material in or on a product for sale;

• you or your organization are **not** the original purchaser of this book.

By following these guidelines you help us keep our products affordable.

Thank you,

Gospel Light

PRAISE FOR YOUTHBUILDERS

I deeply respect and appreciate the groundwork Jim Burns has prepared for true teenage discernment. *YouthBuilders* is timeless in the sense that the framework has made it possible to plug into any society, at any point in time, and to proceed to discuss, experience and arrive at sincere moral and Christian conclusions that will lead to growth and life changes. Reaching young people may be more difficult today than ever before, but God's grace is alive and well in Jim Burns and this wonderful curriculum.

Fr. Angelo J. Artemas, Youth Ministry Director, Greek Orthodox Archdiocese of North and South America

Jim Burns' work represents his integrity and intelligence, along with his heart for kids. *YouthBuilders* will change some lives and save many others.

Stephen Arterburn, Cofounder, The Minirth-Meier New Life Clinic

I heartily recommend Jim Burns' *Youth Builders Group Bible Studies* because they are leader-friendly tools that are ready-to-use in youth groups and Sunday School classes. Jim addresses the tough questions that students are genuinely facing every day and, through his engaging style, challenges young people to make their own decisions to move from their current opinions to God's convictions taught in the Bible. Every youth group will benefit from this excellent curriculum.

Paul Borthwick, Minister of Missions, Grace Chapel

It is about time that someone who knows kids, understands kids and works with kids writes youth curriculum that youth workers, both volunteer and professional, can use. Jim Burns' *YouthBuilders Group Bible Studies* is the curriculum that youth ministry has been waiting a long time for.

Ridge Burns, President, The Center for Student Missions

Jim Burns has found the right balance between learning God's Word and applying it to life. The topics are relevant, up-to-date and on target. Jim gets kids to think. The Parent Page is an extra bonus that continues the teaching in the home and helps involve parents in the process. This is a terrific series, and I highly recommend it.

Les J. Christie, Chair of Youth Ministries Department, San Jose Christian College

There are very few people in the world who know how to communicate life-changing truth effectively to teens. Jim Burns is one of the best. *YouthBuilders Group Bible Studies* puts handles on those skills and makes them available to everyone. These studies are biblically sound, hands-on practical and just plain fun. This one gets a five-star endorsement—which isn't bad since there are only four stars to start with.

Ken Davis, President, Dynamic Communications

I don't know anyone who knows and understands the needs of the youth worker like Jim Burns. His new curriculum not only reveals his knowledge of youth ministry but also his depth and sensitivity to the Scriptures. *YouthBuilders Group Bible Studies* is solid, easy to use and gets students out of their seats and into the Word. I've been waiting for something like this for a long time!

Doug Fields, Pastor of High School, Saddleback Valley Community Church

Jim Burns has a way of being creative without being "hokey." *YouthBuilders Group Bible Studies* take the age-old model of curriculum and gives it a new look with tools such as the Bible *Tuck-in™* and Parent Page. Give this new resource a try and you'll see that Jim shoots straight forward on tough issues. The *YouthBuilders* series is great for leading small group discussions as well as teaching a large class of junior high or high school students. The Parent Page will help you get support from your parents in that they will understand the topics you dealing with in your group. Put Jim's years of experience to work for you by equipping yourself with this quality material.

Curt Gibson, Pastor to Junior High, First Church of the Nazarene of Pasadena

Once again, Jim Burns has managed to handle very timely issues with just the right touch. His *YouthBuilders Group Bible Studies* succeeds in teaching solid, biblical values without being stuffy or preachy. The format is user-friendly, designed to stimulate high involvement and deep discussion. Especially impressive is the Parent Page, a long overdue tool to help parents become part of the Christian education loop. I look forward to using it with my kids!

David M. Hughes, Pastor, First Baptist Church, Winston-Salem

What do you get when you combine a deep love for teens, over 20 years experience in youth ministry and an excellent writer? You get Jim Burns' *YouthBuilders* series! This stuff has absolutely hit the nail on the head. Quality Sunday School and small group material is tough to come by these days, but Jim has put every ounce of creativity he has into these books.

Greg Johnson, author of *Getting Ready for the Guy/Girl Thing* and *Keeping Your Cool While Sharing Your Faith*

Jim Burns has a gift, the gift of combining the relational and theological dynamics of our faith in a graceful, relevant and easy-to-chew-and-swallow way. *YouthBuilders Group Bible Studies* is a hit, not only for teens but for teachers.

Gregg Johnson, National Youth Director, International Church of the Foursquare Gospel

In *YouthBuilders Group Bible Studies*, Jim Burns pulls together the key ingredients for an effective curriculum series. Jim captures the combination of teen involvement, and a solid biblical perspective, with topics that are relevant and straightforward. This series will be a valuable tool in the local church.
Dennis "Tiger" McLuen, Executive Director, Youth Leadership

My ministry takes me to the lost kids in our nation's cities where youth games and activities are often irrelevant and plain Bible knowledge for the sake of learning is unattractive. Young people need the information necessary to make wise decisions related to everyday problems. *YouthBuilders* will help many young people integrate their faith into everyday life, which after all is our goal as youth workers.
Miles McPherson, President, Project Intercept

Finally, a Bible study that has it all! It's action-packed, practical and biblical; but that's only the beginning. *YouthBuilders* involves students in the Scriptures. It's relational, interactive and leads kids towards lifestyle changes. The unique aspect is a page for parents, something that's usually missing from adolescent curriculum. Jim Burns has outdone himself. This isn't a homerun—it's a grand-slam!
Dr. David Olshine, Director of Youth Ministries, Columbia International University

Here is a thoughtful and relevant curriculum designed to meet the needs of youth workers, parents and students. It's creative, interactive and biblical—and with Jim Burns' name on it, you know you're getting a quality resource.
Laurie Polich, Youth Director, First Presbyterian Church of Berkeley

Jim Burns has done a fantastic job of putting together a youth curriculum that will work. *YouthBuilders* provides the motivation and information for leaders and the types of experience and content that will capture junior high and high school people. I recommend it highly.
Denny Rydberg, President, Young Life

In 10 years of youth ministry I've never used a curriculum because I've never found anything that actively involves students in the learning process, speaks to young people where they are and challenges them with biblical truth—I'll use this! *YouthBuilders Group Bible Studies* is a complete curriculum that is helpful to parents, youth leaders and, most importantly, today's youth.
Glenn Schroeder, Youth and Young Adult Ministries, Vineyard Christian Fellowship, Anaheim

This new material by Jim Burns represents a vitality in curriculum and, I believe, a more mature and faithful direction. *YouthBuilders Group Bible Studies* challenges youth by teaching them how to make decisions rather than telling them what decisions to make. Each session offers teaching concepts, presents options and asks for a decision. I believe it's healthy, the way Christ taught and represents the abilities, personhood and faithfulness of youth. I give it an A+!
J. David Stone, President, Stone & Associates

Jim Burns has done it again! This is a practical, timely and reality-based resource for equipping teens to live life in the fast-paced, pressure-packed adolescent world of the 90s. A very refreshing creative oasis in the curriculum desert!
Rich Van Pelt, President, Alongside Ministries

I couldn't be more excited about the *YouthBuilders Group Bible Studies*. It couldn't have arrived at a more needed time. Spiritually we approach the future engaged in war with young people taking direct hits from the devil. This series will practically help teens who feel partially equipped to "put on the whole armor of God."
Mike MacIntosh, Pastor, Horizon Christian Fellowship

Jim Burns' *YouthBuilders Group Bible Studies* will be a tremendous ministry resource for years to come. Jim's years of experience and love for kids are evident on every page. This is a resource that is user-friendly, learner-centered and intentionally biblical. I love having a resource like this that I can recommend to youth ministry volunteers and professionals! I especially like the idea of adding a Parent Page in each session. Neat idea!
Duffy Robbins, Chairman, Department of Youth Ministry, Eastern College

The practicing youth worker always needs more ammunition. Here is a whole book full of practical, usable resources for those facing kids face-to-face. *YouthBuilders Group Bible Studies* will get that blank stare off the faces of kids in your youth meeting!
Jay Kesler, President, Taylor University

YouthBuilders Group Bible Studies is a tremendous new set of resources for reaching students. Jim has his finger on the pulse of youth today. He understands their mind-sets, and has prepared these studies in a way that will capture their attentions and lead to greater maturity in Christ. I heartily recommend these studies.
Rick Warren, Senior Pastor, Saddleback Valley Community Church

DEDICATION

To Ron Spence

Thank you, Ron, for believing in the vision to reach young people through THIS SIDE UP. Thank you for all the fun you have brought to our ministry. Thank you for all the quiet, behind the scenes ways you support me as a friend. Thank you for your incredible prayers.

"Praise the Lord! The church people are here."

Your brother in Christ,

Jim

C O N T E N T S

THANKS AND THANKS AGAIN!

This project is definitely a team effort. First of all, thank you to Cathy, Christy, Rebecca and Heidi Burns, the women of my life.

Thank you to Jill Corey, my incredible assistant and long-time friend.

Thank you to Doug Webster for your outstanding job as executive director of the National Institute of Youth Ministry (NIYM).

Thank you to the NIYM staff in San Clemente: Teresa Parsons, Gary Lenhart, Roger Royster, Ron Spence, Luchi Bierbower, Dean Bruns, Laurie Pilz, Ken Bayard, Russ Cline and Larry Acosta.

Thank you to our 150-plus associate trainers who have been my coworkers, friends and sacrificial guinea pigs.

Thank you to Kyle Duncan, Bill Greig III and Jean Daly for convincing me that Gospel Light is a great publisher who deeply believes in the mission to reach kids. I believe!

Thank you to the Youth Specialties world. Tic, Mike and Wayne, so many years ago, you brought on a wet-behind-the-ears youth worker with hair and taught me most everything I know about youth work today.

Thank you to the hundreds of donors, supporters and friends of NIYM. You are helping create an international grassroots movement that is helping young people make positive decisions that will affect them for the rest of their lives.

"When there is no counsel, the people fall; But in the multitude of counselors there is safety"
(Proverbs 11:14, *NKJV*)

Jim Burns
San Clemente, CA

YouthBuilders Group Bible Studies

It's Relational—Students learn best when they talk not when you talk. There is always a get acquainted section in the Warm Up. All the experiences are based on building community in your group.

It's Biblical—With no apologies, this series in unashamedly Christian. Every session has a practical, relevant Bible study.

It's Experiential—Studies show that young people retain up to 85 percent of the material when they are *involved* in action-oriented, experiential learning. The sessions use role plays, discussion starters, case studies, graphs and other experiential, educational methods. *We believe it's a sin to bore a teen with the gospel.*

It's Interactive—This study is geared to get students feeling comfortable with sharing ideas and interacting with peers and leaders.

It's Easy to Follow—The sessions have been prepared by Jim Burns to allow the leader to pick up the material and use it. There is little preparation time on your part. Jim did the work for you.

It's Adaptable—You can pick and choose from several topics or go straight through the material as a whole study.

It's Parent Oriented—The Parent Page helps you to do youth ministry at it's finest. Christian education should take place in the home as well as in the church. The Parent Page is your chance to come alongside the parents and help them have a good discussion with their kids.

It's Proven—This material was not written by someone in an ivory tower. It was written for, and has already been used with, teens. They love it.

How to Use This Study

The 12 sessions are divided into three stand-alone units. Each unit has four sessions. You may choose to teach all 12 sessions consecutively. Or you may use only one unit. Or you may present individual sessions. You know your group best so you choose.

Each of the 12 sessions is divided into five sections.

Warm Up—Young people will stay in your youth group if they feel comfortable and make friends in the group. This section is designed for you and the students to get to know each other better. These activities are filled with history-giving and affirming questions and experiences.

Team Effort—Following the model of Jesus, the Master Teacher, these activities engage teens in the session. Stories, group situations, surveys and more bring the session to the students. There is an option for junior high/middle school students and one for high school students.

In the Word—Most young people are biblically illiterate. These Bible studies present the Word of God and encourage students to see the relevance of the Scriptures to their lives.

Things to Think About—Young people need the opportunity to really think through

the issues at hand. These discussion starters get students talking about the subject and interacting on important issues.

Parent Page—A youth worker can only do so much. Reproduce this page and get it into the hands of parents. This tool allows quality parent/teen communication that really brings the session home.

THE BIBLE *TUCK-IN*™

It's a tear-out sheet you fold and place in your Bible, containing the essentials you'll need for teaching your group.

HERE'S HOW TO USE IT:

To prepare for the session, first study the session. Tear out the Bible *Tuck-In*™ and personalize it by making notes. Fold the Bible *Tuck-In*™ in half on the dotted line. Slip it into your Bible for easy reference throughout the session. The Key Verse, Biblical Basis and Big Idea at the beginning of the Bible *Tuck-In*™ will help you keep the session on track. With the Bible *Tuck-In*™ your students will see that your teaching comes from the Bible and won't be distracted by a leader's guide.

PRAYER: COMMUNICATION WITH GOD

LEADER'S PEP TALK

Before I started this curriculum project, I asked over 150 of my associates at the National Institute of Youth Ministry to give me their desires for subjects for the *YouthBuilders Group Bible Studies*. *The number one requested subject was prayer.* How interesting it is that a regular part of most every youth meeting and every worship service is prayer, but we rarely ever talk about it in our youth groups, Christian schools or even family devotions. Yet as William Carey once wrote, "Prayer—secret, fervent, believing prayer—lies at the root of all personal godliness."

I am really glad you picked up this study because on the following pages your students, and hopefully you, will be introduced to the depth and breadth of the role that prayer plays in our spiritual lives. It's hard to just talk about prayer without praying. That's why I have included many opportunities for prayer and worship throughout the study. Experiential education says don't just talk about it, do it.

I believe you are in for a real spiritual treat because when all is said and done prayer is simply communication with God. There isn't anything you can do that is more important than helping your students begin or continue the process of building a relationship of communication with the Creator, Savior and Sustainer of their lives.

Although prayer was the most requested subject from the youth workers, I doubt the students would have voted it number one. As you know, at camp the class on prayer has a handful of faithful and the class on sex, drugs and rock and roll is standing room only. That's okay, and this study won't automatically change that trend. However, our job in this study is to get young people talking with God, to keep them talking to Him and have them enter into a deeper form of communication than ever before. On a side note, let's help them begin to appreciate worship in a new and fresh way.

As you investigate this section on Prayer: Communication with God, remember that your sessions may not have the highs and laughs of other topical curriculum. Yet, you are about to introduce your students to what may be closest to the heart of God: true communication with Him.

Thank you, my dear friend, for tackling the subject of prayer and thank you for introducing the power of prayer to students. It's a life-changing topic.

PRAYER: COMMUNICATION WITH GOD

Key Verse

"In the morning, O LORD, you hear my voice; in the morning I lay my requests before you and wait in expectation."
Psalm 5:3

Biblical Basis

Psalm 5:3; 9:1,2;
Matthew 7:7;
Mark 9:7;
1 Thessalonians 5:18;
1 John 1:9

The Big Idea

Communication with God is what prayer is all about. A consistent prayer life will develop a deeper, more intimate relationship with God.

Aims of This Session

During this session you will guide students to:
- Examine what prayer is;
- Discover how prayer works;
- Implement an understanding of the elements of prayer.

Warm Up

A True Story—
A look at prayer through the eyes of a child.

Team Effort— Junior High/ Middle School

Things That Block Communication with God—
A survey of challenges to their prayer lives.

Team Effort— High School

Woman Says Prayer Helped Her Win Lottery—
A discussion of what to pray for.

In the Word

What Is Prayer?—
A Bible study on the different elements of prayer.

Things to Think About (OPTIONAL)

Questions to get students thinking and talking about communicating with God.

Parent Page

A tool to get the session into the home and allow parents and young people to discuss a relationship with God based on communication.

LEADER'S DEVOTIONAL

The word "prayer" may bring reactions from the young people you teach that range from "I can't do it!" to "I never think about it!" They may find it hard to believe that anyone *really* has a prayer life or relationship with God that goes beyond what they see in the outward action of church events.

Where could young people get such a notion? Could it be from the (gulp!) adults around them? They see us interact with each other and with them. But how do most young people *know* if an adult ever interacts with *God*? Sure, pastors and Sunday School teachers talk about God. Prayers are said at the beginning and end of every church activity, but all too often, prayer and intimacy with God are either dealt with in abstract terms—or not at all.

Prayer is the power, the life-changing element that creates passionate drive and immense change in the lives of people who seek God. We do it in private, and we seem to keep it "in the closet" when it comes to really talking about it. Why is it so difficult to make our prayer lives public? Are we afraid that our students (or we) will get too fanatic? Or is it that when it comes to talking about our experiences, we really don't have that much to talk about?

That's where this lesson begins. When your intimacy with God becomes so exciting that your excitement spills over into the information this course provides, your young people will begin to learn, not just hear!

If you want to see the students you teach light up when they talk about real answers God has given them to their prayers, if you want to see them realize that they can go way beyond the "Now I lay me down to sleep" level of prayer that paralyzes much of Christendom, if there is even a spark of longing in your heart to see God make your own prayer life more powerful, more intimate, more life-changing, you're on the right track! Give God all He wants of your prayer life.

Adults who eagerly evidence that they have been with God, who comfortably talk about His powerful answers to prayer in their own lives, will take intimacy with God from the realm of the theoretical to the actual for young people. You can be the adult who proves to your students by your own life that intimacy with God is possible, real and life-changing! (Mary Gross, editor, Gospel Light.)

"Prayer is friendship with God. Friendship is not formal, but it is not formless: it has its cultivation, its behavior, its obligations, even its disciplines; and the casual mind kills it."—

George Arthur Buttrick, *Prayer* (Abingdon-Cokesbury, 1942)

PRAYER: COMMUNICATION WITH GOD

KEY VERSE

"In the morning, O LORD, you hear my voice; in the morning I lay my requests before you and wait in expectation." Psalm 5:3

BIBLICAL BASIS

Psalm 5:3; 9:1,2; Matthew 7:7; Mark 9:7; 1 Thessalonians 5:18; 1 John 1:9

THE BIG IDEA

Communication with God is what prayer is all about. A consistent prayer life will develop a deeper, more intimate relationship with God.

WARM UP (5-10 MINUTES)
A TRUE STORY

- Display a copy of "A True Story" on page 23 using an overhead projector.
- Read aloud the story.
- As a whole group, discuss how to describe prayer to five-year-old Josh. List ideas on a chalkboard or overhead.

  Todd and Charlotte have a wonderful son named Josh. He is five years old and quite a character. One night Josh wouldn't go to bed. He was scared because his mom was sick, and he didn't want to be in his room by himself. Todd had tried it all: a glass of water, bathroom visits, the light left on, reading another story, bribing, anger and jokes. Basically his last choice was prayer.

  He said to little Josh, "See that picture of Jesus above your bed? Let's ask Jesus to be with you in the room while you sleep. He will watch over you and protect you."

  Josh looked at the picture and looked at his dad. "Okay," he said through his tears. They prayed. Josh kept his eyes peeled on the picture of Jesus. When they finished praying, Todd thought it worked. Josh was quiet.

  However, 15 minutes later Josh started screaming at the top of his lungs, "Daddy, Daddy come quickly." Todd again went up to Josh's room. This time Josh asked, "Dad, can you ask Jesus to leave my bedroom? He's keeping me awake!"

TEAM EFFORT—JUNIOR HIGH/ MIDDLE SCHOOL (15-20 MINUTES)

THINGS THAT BLOCK COMMUNICATION WITH GOD

- Give each student a copy of "Things That Block Communication with God" on page 25 and a pen or pencil.
- Students individually complete the page.

Fold

---

4. Matthew 7:7
(Asking.)
5. Mark 9:7
(Listening.)
6. Write a definition of your element of prayer.

7. Write a prayer of your particular element.

8. Describe why your element of prayer is important.

SO WHAT?

1. What are other elements of prayer not mentioned in this section?

2. Are all these elements of prayer necessary for a well-rounded life of prayer? Why or why not?

3. Which elements of prayer do you need to place a special emphasis on in your life? Five Minutes with God

   Prayer is best learned by practice. As a group, take a few moments to pray together.
   - Praise
   - Thanksgiving
   - Confession
   - Asking
   - Listening

THINGS TO THINK ABOUT (OPTIONAL)

- Use the questions on page 33 after or as a part of "In the Word."
1. How is prayer different than a face-to-face conversation?

2. Name three ways prayer can bring you closer to God.

3. How can prayer be a dialogue with God rather than a monologue?

PARENT PAGE

- Distribute page to parents.

- Divide students into pairs. Have students share how they will overcome their challenges. Here is a list of potential prayer blockers. Read the list and identify the ones that give you the most problems in your prayer life.

	Often	Sometimes	Seldom
1. Lack of discipline	☐	☐	☐
2. Not making prayer a priority	☐	☐	☐
3. Falling asleep while praying	☐	☐	☐
4. Hectic schedule	☐	☐	☐
5. Don't feel God's presence	☐	☐	☐
6. Guilt	☐	☐	☐
7. Lack of faith that He is listening	☐	☐	☐
8. Doubting His existence	☐	☐	☐
9. Selfishness	☐	☐	☐
10. Frustration in prayer	☐	☐	☐
11. Daydreaming	☐	☐	☐

Write down a couple of these blocks you would like to work on eliminating from your prayer life. Write out how you will begin to overcome this challenge. (Example: Hectic schedule—Pray every morning at 7:00 A.M., talk less on the phone.)

....

....

Team Effort—High School (15-20 Minutes)

Woman Says Prayer Helped Her Win Lottery

- Divide students into groups of three or four.
- Give each student a copy of "Woman Says Prayer Helped Her Win Lottery" on page 27 and a pen or pencil.
- Read aloud the account.
- Students discuss questions.
- As a whole group, discuss the responses to Prayer Possibilities.

As far as Regina Hammond is concerned, luck has little to do with it. The 37-year-old flight attendant won $100,000 in a Colorado lottery game, on top of $50,000 she won the previous year the same way. And she's not finished yet. Her goal is the $1 million grand prize. Hammond believes that prayer has paved her way to riches. "I pray to God to help me and He answers," she says.

Fold
---

1. How does Regina Hammond's claim make you feel? If prayer works, why don't all lottery players pray and win? Do you think Hammond will win the million dollars? Why or why not?

2. Should people pray to get rich? To win sports events? To be successful? Explain.

....

3. Some people feel lotteries are illegal and sinful. If that's true, why would God answer Hammond's prayers to win? Would you pray to win a lottery? Why or why not?

....

Prayer Possibilities
Check the items you'd feel comfortable praying for. Give reasons for your answers.
I'd pray for:

.... an A on a test.

.... lots of money.

.... getting a job.

.... a better complexion.

.... winning a game.

.... new clothes.

.... not getting caught drinking.

.... getting a date.

.... losing or gaining weight.

....

....

In the Word (25-30 Minutes)

What Is Prayer?

- Give each student a copy of "What Is Prayer?" on pages 29 and 31 and a pen or pencil.
- Students complete the Bible study.
- Divide students into five groups. Assign each group one element of prayer to complete items 6–8.
- As a whole group, complete Five Minutes with God. Lead the group in one minute of prayer for each of the five elements.

Read each of these verses. What element of prayer do you find in the verse?

1. Psalm 9:1,2
(Praise.)

2. 1 Thessalonians 5:18
(Thanksgiving.)

3. 1 John 1:9
(Confession.)

WARM UP

A TRUE STORY

Todd and Charlotte have a wonderful son named Josh. He is five years old and quite a character. One night Josh wouldn't go to bed. He was scared because his mom was sick, and he didn't want to be in his room by himself. Todd had tried it all: a glass of water, bathroom visits, the light left on, reading another story, bribing, anger and jokes. Basically his last choice was prayer.

He said to little Josh, "See that picture of Jesus above your bed? Let's ask Jesus to be with you in the room while you sleep. He will watch over you and protect you."

Josh looked at the picture and looked at his dad. "Okay," he said through his tears. They prayed. Josh kept his eyes peeled on the picture of Jesus. When they finished praying, Todd thought it worked. Josh was quiet.

However, 15 minutes later Josh started screaming at the top of his lungs, "Daddy, Daddy come quickly." Todd again went up to Josh's room. This time Josh asked, "Dad, can you ask Jesus to leave my bedroom? He's keeping me awake!"

TEAM EFFORT

THINGS THAT BLOCK COMMUNICATION WITH GOD

Here is a list of potential prayer blockers. Read the list and identify the ones that give you the most problems in your prayer life.

		Often	Sometimes	Seldom
1.	Lack of discipline	☐	☐	☐
2.	Not making prayer a priority	☐	☐	☐
3.	Falling asleep while praying	☐	☐	☐
4.	Hectic schedule	☐	☐	☐
5.	Don't feel God's presence	☐	☐	☐
6.	Guilt	☐	☐	☐
7.	Lack of faith that He is listening	☐	☐	☐
8.	Doubting His existence	☐	☐	☐
9.	Selfishness	☐	☐	☐
10.	Frustration in prayer	☐	☐	☐
11.	Daydreaming	☐	☐	☐

Write down a couple of these blocks you would like to work on eliminating from your prayer life. Write out how you will begin to overcome this potential problem. (Example: Hectic schedule—Pray every morning at 7:00 A.M., talk less on the phone.)

....

....

....

....

....

....

....

....

TEAM **E**FFORT

WOMAN **S**AYS **P**RAYER **H**ELPED **H**ER **W**IN **L**OTTERY[1]

As far as Regina Hammond is concerned, luck has little to do with it. The 37-year-old flight attendant won $100,000 in a Colorado lottery game, on top of $50,000 she won the previous year the same way. And she's not finished yet. Her goal is the $1 million grand prize.

Hammond believes that prayer has paved her way to riches. "I pray to God to help me and he answers," she says.

1. How does Regina Hammond's claim make you feel? If prayer works, why don't all lottery players pray and win? Do you think Hammond will win the million dollars? Why or why not?

....

....

....

2. Should people pray to get rich? To win sports events? To be successful? Explain.

....

....

....

3. Some people feel lotteries are illegal and sinful. If that's true, why would God answer Hammond's prayers to win? Would you pray to win a lottery? Why or why not?

....

....

....

Prayer Possibilities

Check the items you'd feel comfortable praying for. Give reasons for your answers.

I'd pray for:

...... an *A* on a test.

...... lots of money.

...... getting a job.

...... a better complexion.

...... winning a game.

...... new clothes.

...... not getting caught drinking.

...... getting a date.

...... losing or gaining weight.

Note

1. "Woman Says Prayer Helped Her Win Lottery,"
Headline News Discussion Starters
(Loveland, CO: Group, 1990), pp. 30-31.
Used by permission.

27

 **IN THE WORD**

WHAT IS PRAYER?

Read each of these verses. What element of prayer do you find in the verse?

1. Psalm 9:1,2

2. 1 Thessalonians 5:18

3. 1 John 1:9

4. Matthew 7:7

5. Mark 9:7

6. Write a definition of your element of prayer.

7. Write a prayer of your particular element.

8. Describe why your element of prayer is important.

29

So What?

1. What are other elements of prayer not mentioned in this section?

....

....

....

2. Are all these elements of prayer necessary for a well-rounded life of prayer? Why or why not?

....

....

....

3. Which elements of prayer do you need to place a special emphasis on in your life?

....

....

....

Five Minutes with God

Prayer is best learned by practice. As a group take a few moments to pray together.

- Praise
- Thanksgiving
- Confession
- Asking
- Listening

Things to Think About

1. How is prayer different from a face-to-face conversation?

....

....

....

2. Name three ways prayer can bring you closer to God.

....

....

....

3. How can prayer be a dialogue with God rather than a monologue?

....

....

....

....

PARENT PAGE

PRAYER: COMMUNICATION WITH GOD

Prayer is communication with God giving us the opportunity to share our lives with Him. When we are in communication with God, we begin to understand the riches of His kingdom. Failure to have consistent communication with God often shuts the door to God's work in our lives. But remember, even with more knowledge about the subject of prayer, the truth of the matter is the only way to improve your communication with God is to practice going to Him in prayer. And the bottom line is: Prayer is communication with God. In Christ you have the privilege of coming into the presence of God and talking *with* Him. Prayer is dialogue with God.

POPCORN PRAYERS

Take a few minutes together to pray a word or a phrase expressing to God how you feel about your relationship with Him and communicating with Him. Pray whatever word or phrase comes to your mind.

Session 1 "Prayer: Communication with God" Date ....

THE PRAYER OF RELINQUISHMENT

KEY VERSES

"Then Jesus went with his disciples to a place called Gethsemane, and he said to them, 'Sit here while I go over there and pray.' He took Peter and the two sons of Zebedee along with him, and he began to be sorrowful and troubled. Then he said to them, 'My soul is overwhelmed with sorrow to the point of death. Stay here and keep watch with me.'

"Going a little farther, he fell with his face to the ground and prayed, 'My Father, if it is possible, may this cup be taken from me. Yet not as I will, but as you will.'

"Then he returned to his disciples and found them sleeping. 'Could you men not keep watch with me for one hour?' he asked Peter. 'Watch and pray so that you will not fall into temptation. The spirit is willing, but the body is weak.'

"He went away a second time and prayed, 'My Father, if it is not possible for this cup to be taken away unless I drink it, may your will be done.'

"When he came back, he again found them sleeping, because their eyes were heavy. So he left them and went away once more and prayed the third time, saying the same thing.

"Then he returned to the disciples and said to them, 'Are you still sleeping and resting? Look, the hour is near, and the Son of Man is betrayed into the hands of sinners. Rise, let us go! Here comes my betrayer!'" Matthew 26:36-46

BIBLICAL BASIS

Matthew 26:36-46;
John 14:21;
Philippians 2:5-11;
Galatians 2:20

THE BIG IDEA

The prayer of relinquishment is a prayer of absolute surrender of your will to God's will. The result is freedom and spiritual growth.

AIMS OF THIS SESSION

During this session you will guide students to:
- Examine the prayer of relinquishment;
- Discover freedom and spiritual growth through the prayer of relinquishment;
- Implement actual prayers of relinquishment to God.

WARM UP

Your Last Days—
Young people share how they would spend their last days.

TEAM EFFORT— JUNIOR HIGH/ MIDDLE SCHOOL

$3.00 Worth of God—
Students examine where they need to surrender to God.

TEAM EFFORT— HIGH SCHOOL

Tom Meets God—
A skit of a young man encountering his shortcomings before God.

IN THE WORD

The School at Gethsemane—
A Bible study on Jesus' ultimate surrendering.

THINGS TO THINK ABOUT (OPTIONAL)

Questions to get students thinking and talking about relinquishment.

PARENT PAGE

A tool to get the session into the home and allow parents and young people to discuss relinquishing through obedience to God.

37

LEADER'S DEVOTIONAL

Negotiation is a way of life for most of us. We give a little; the other party gives a little; everyone is satisfied. This is the way the world works. It is not, however, the way God works! God is not the Great Negotiator in the Sky. His love is unconditional. His holiness is complete and perfect—and His demands are absolute.

There was once a woman who tried desperately to negotiate with God. She was willing to give Him everything but five percent. "Just five percent!" became her mental battle cry. After all, she was teaching Sunday School, helping with the youth group, taking her turn at nursery duty, organizing fund-raisers and...the list went on and on. But God simply does not negotiate. He did not want her Christian activity, her busyness. He wanted all of her. Ninety-five percent was not enough. And trying to hold on to that five percent nearly destroyed her.

"Absolute surrender" is a term we don't hear very often anymore, simply because the world views negotiation as a great good, which it is, in its place. Its place, however, is not with God. Absolute surrender of every single thing we are, what we hope, dream or want, must be laid at His feet. This is not a one-shot deal, either. It has less to do with one trip to the altar than with saying every single day, "God, I am Yours. All I have, all I want to keep for myself, that little five percent, is Yours. I take my hands off completely. Do what pleases You!" This is all God asks. Because when you are completely surrendered, His Spirit can move in and make you able to grow fruit, flow with love, as was never possible with that ninety-five percent loaded up with Christian busyness!

What keeps you from absolute surrender? Whatever it is, give it up. Until you yourself have made that step, in all honesty and humility, you will not be able to teach it to your students. The struggle is worth it and the result is glorious! (Mary Gross, editor, Gospel Light.)

"The self of instinct has missed its way. It carries a load of sin, of lust, of dishonesty, of falsehood, of physical heredity which from God's viewpoint is enmity to him. [In the prayer of Gethsemane] all this Christ resolutely flung aside"—

Toyohiko Kagawa,
Meditations of the Cross
(Willett Clark, 1935)

THE PRAYER OF RELINQUISHMENT

KEY VERSES

"Then Jesus went with his disciples to a place called Gethsemane, and he said to them, 'Sit here while I go over there and pray.' He took Peter and the two sons of Zebedee along with him, and he began to be sorrowful and troubled. Then he said to them, 'My soul is overwhelmed with sorrow to the point of death. Stay here and keep watch with me.'

"Going a little farther, he fell with his face to the ground and prayed, 'My Father, if it is possible, may this cup be taken from me. Yet not as I will, but as you will.'

"Then he returned to his disciples and found them sleeping. 'Could you men not keep watch with me for one hour?' he asked Peter. 'Watch and pray so that you will not fall into temptation. The spirit is willing, but the body is weak.'

"He went away a second time and prayed, 'My Father, if it is not possible for this cup to be taken away unless I drink it, may your will be done.'

"When he came back, he again found them sleeping, because their eyes were heavy. So he left them and went away once more and prayed the third time, saying the same thing.

"Then he returned to the disciples and said to them, 'Are you still sleeping and resting? Look, the hour is near, and the Son of Man is betrayed into the hands of sinners. Rise, let us go! Here comes my betrayer!'" Matthew 26:36-46

BIBLICAL BASIS

Matthew 26:36-46; John 14:21; Philippians 2:5-11; Galatians 2:20

THE BIG IDEA

The prayer of relinquishment is a prayer of absolute surrender of your will to God's will. The result is freedom and spiritual growth.

WARM UP (5-10 MINUTES)

YOUR LAST DAYS

• Display a copy of "Your Last Days" on page 41 using an overhead projector.
• Divide students into groups of three or four.
• Students discuss question.

If you had only a few days to live, what would you do with your time? Choose one or more of the following and tell why.

_____ Throw a party.
_____ Watch television.
_____ Spend time with my family or closest friends.

What would be the results of a life of relinquishment?

Relinquishment is no easy task. Even Jesus struggled. It took three times to pray the same prayer, and He even had a bloody sweat lasting long into the night. If you struggle with releasing your will to the Lord then you are in good company.

- Abraham had to release his son Isaac. (See Genesis 22.)
- Moses released his will for the sake of Israel and Egypt. (See Exodus 4; 7:1-6.)
- David released his will for the son given by Bathsheba. (See 2 Samuel 12:16-22.)
- Paul released his desire to be free of his "thorn in the flesh." (See 2 Corinthians 12:1-10.)

SO WHAT?

What part of your life is God calling you to give over to Him through a prayer of relinquishment? Don't let another minute go by without praying that prayer. If you struggle, you're in good company, but as an act of submission, now is the time to experience freedom and release.

THINGS TO THINK ABOUT (OPTIONAL)

• Use the questions on page 51 after or as a part of "In the Word."

1. How does the battle of spirit and flesh relate to the prayer of relinquishment?

2. Why is the prayer of relinquishment described as a release to freedom?

3. How does Galatians 2:20, "I have been crucified with Christ and I no longer live, but Christ lives in me. The life I live in the body, I live by faith in the Son of God, who loved me and gave himself for me," fit into the theme of a prayer of relinquishment?

PARENT PAGE

• Distribute page to parents.

Travel to a place I have always wanted to go.

Do nothing different.

Work hard to meet a girlfriend or boyfriend.

Plan my funeral.

Pray like crazy.

TEAM EFFORT—JUNIOR HIGH/MIDDLE SCHOOL (15-20 MINUTES)

TOM MEETS GOD

- Assign the skit roles.
- Give each performer a copy of "Tom Meets God" on page 43. If possible, do this before the session so performers have an opportunity to rehearse.
- Students perform skit.

TEAM EFFORT—HIGH SCHOOL (15-20 MINUTES)

$3.00 WORTH OF GOD

- Divide students into groups of three or four.
- Give each student a copy of "$3.00 Worth of God" on page 45 and a pen or pencil, or display a copy using an overhead projector.
- Students complete the page.

Far too often Christians act like the person in this story:

"I would like to buy $3 worth of God, please. Not enough to explode my soul or disturb my sleep, but just enough to equal a cup of warm milk or a snooze in the sunshine....I want ecstasy, not transformation; I want the warmth of the womb not a new birth. I want a pound of the Eternal in a paper sack. I would like to buy $3 worth of God, please."

What is the key principle in this story?

List three areas of your life in which you need to be more surrendered to God. (Be specific.)

1. ....

2. ....

3. ....

IN THE WORD (25-30 MINUTES)

THE SCHOOL AT GETHSEMANE

- Divide students into groups of three or four.
- Give each student a copy of "The School at Gethsemane" on pages 47 and 49 and a pen or pencil.
- Students complete the Bible study.

An inductive Bible study on one of the great secrets of the faith.

The Scripture: Matthew 26:36-46

1. **Who?**
   a. **What is taking place?**
   (Jesus, Peter and the two sons of Zebedee, James and John.)
   b. **Who wrote it?**
   (Matthew.)

2. **What?**
   a. **What is taking place?**
   (Jesus is praying before His arrest and crucifixion.)
   b. **How many times did Christ ask God to remove the cup?**
   (Three times.)
   c. **What was the "cup"?**
   (His imminent suffering and death.)
   d. **What is the prayer of relinquishment?**
   (Praying for God's will to be done.)

3. **Where?**
   Where is it happening?
   (Gethsemane.)

4. **When?**
   When in this event in the total life of Jesus on earth?
   (Just before His death.)

5. **Why?**
   a. **Why does Jesus pray the prayer of relinquishment?**
   (He has submitted Himself to God's will. He knows that through His death and resurrection He can offer us salvation.)
   b. **Are there consequences to this prayer? What are they?**
   (Yes. Jesus is arrested, whipped and killed.)

6. **Well?**
   How does this prayer apply to your life?

Jesus said, "Father, if you are willing, take this cup from me; yet not my will, but yours be done" (Luke 22:42), Richard Foster calls the prayer of relinquishment a prayer of:
   – self-emptying
   – surrender
   – abandonment
   – release
   – reservation

How do these principles make sense in this account of Jesus?

How can you use this account in your own life?

Fold

WARM UP

YOUR LAST DAYS

If you had only a few days to live, what would you do with your time? Choose one or more of the following and tell why.

.... Throw a party.

.... Watch television.

.... Spend time with my family or closest friends.

.... Travel to a place I have always wanted to go.

.... Do nothing different.

.... Work hard to meet a girlfriend or boyfriend.

.... Plan my funeral.

.... Pray like crazy.

....

TEAM EFFORT

TOM MEETS GOD[1]

Tom: (Knocks and an angel opens the door). Hi! My name is Tom. I would like to see the person in charge, please.

Angel: Sure, come on in.

Tom: Look, aaa, I know this guy is really important, but do you think he would see someone like me?

Angel: He sees everyone. You can see him any time you'd like.

Tom: Could I see him now?

Angel: Go right on in.

Tom: Now?

Angel: Yes.

Tom: (Hesitating and then slowly walking in). Uh, excuse me, my name is Tom. I wondered if I could see You for a few minutes?

God: My name is God and I've got all the time you need.

Tom: Well, I'm going to high school right now, and I am a little confused about what I should do. A couple of my friends say You can help, but they seem just as confused as I am. To be quite honest, I haven't really been impressed by Your work. I mean, don't get me wrong, my friends are really good friends, you know, and they really seem to like me, but, they haven't got it so good. Bob, one of my friends, has a dad that is an alcoholic and my other friend's folks are getting a divorce. The crazy thing is my folks are great. I really love them. Everything's going great...except...except I can't seem to see the point in life. In spite of all the junk that is happening to my friends, they really seem to be convinced that You are important. So that's why I'm here. I just thought You could give me some pointers. I just feel kinda lost.

God: My price is high.

Tom: That's okay, because my folks are pretty well off. What is it?

God: All.

Tom: All?

God: Yes, all. Everything.

Tom: Sheesh. Don't You have a layaway plan? How about a pay-as-you-go plan? Isn't your profit margin a little out of line?

God: Actually, My cost was quite high also...ask My Son.

Tom: Well, uh, I think I'll have to wait a while. I appreciate You taking the time to talk to me and I'm sure You're worth it. It's just that at my age, it's a little too soon to give up everything. After all, when you're young, that's when the good times happen. Besides, I think I can get what I'm looking for at a much cheaper price.

God: Be careful, Tom. The price may be cheaper, but your cost may be much higher than you think.

Tom: Yeah, sure. Well, nice talking to You, God. Maybe I'll see You around some time.

God: Yes, Tom, and there's no maybe about it.

Note

1. Adapted from "Tom Meets God," *Ideas 17-20* (El Cajon, CA: Youth Specialties), pp. 141-142. Used by permission.

TEAM EFFORT

$3.00 WORTH OF GOD

Far too often Christians act like the person in this story:

"I would like to buy $3.00 worth of God, please. Not enough to explode my soul or disturb my sleep, but just enough to equal a cup of warm milk or a snooze in the sunshine....I want ecstasy, not transformation; I want the warmth of the womb not a new birth. I want a pound of the Eternal in a paper sack. I would like to buy $3 worth of God, please."[1]

What is the key principle in this story?

....

....

List three areas of your life in which you need to be more surrendered to God. (Be specific.)

1...

....

....

....

2...

....

....

....

3...

....

....

....

....

Note

1. Wilbur Rees, "$3.00 Worth of God," source unknown.

 **IN THE WORD**

THE SCHOOL AT GETHSEMANE

An inductive Bible study on one of the great secrets of the faith.

The Scripture: Matthew 26:36-46

1. Who?
   a. What persons are involved in this Scripture?

   b. Who wrote it?

2. What?
   a. What is taking place?

   b. How many times did Christ ask God to remove the cup?

   c. What was the "cup"?

   d. What is the prayer of relinquishment?

3. Where?
   Where is it happening?

4. When?
   When is this event in the total life of Jesus on earth?

5. Why?
   a. Why does Jesus pray the prayer of relinquishment?

   b. Are there consequences to this prayer? What are they?

6. Well?
   How does this prayer apply to your life?

Jesus said, "Father, if you are willing, take this cup from me; yet not my will, but yours be done" (Luke 22:42). Richard Foster calls the prayer of relinquishment a prayer of:
- self-emptying
- surrender
- abandonment
- release
- reservation[1]

47

How do these principles make sense in this account of Jesus?

....

....

....

How can you use this account in your own life?

....

....

....

What would be the results of a life of relinquishment?

....

....

Relinquishment is no easy task. Even Jesus struggled. It took three times to pray the same prayer, and He even had a bloody sweat lasting long into the night. If you struggle with releasing your will to the Lord then you are in good company.

- Abraham had to release his son Isaac. (See Genesis 22.)
- Moses released his will for the sake of Israel and Egypt. (See Exodus 4; 7:1-6.)
- David released his will for the son given by Bathsheba. (See 2 Samuel 12:16-22.)
- Paul released his desire to be free of his "thorn in the flesh." (See 2 Corinthians 12:7-10.)

So WHAT?

What part of your life is God calling you to give over to Him through a prayer of relinquishment?

....

....

Don't let another minute go by without praying that prayer. If you struggle, you're in good company, but as an act of submission, now is the time to experience freedom and release.

Note

1. Richard J. Foster, *Prayer: Finding the Heart's True Home* (San Francisco, CA: Harper Collins, 1992), pp. 47-56.

THINGS TO **T**HINK **A**BOUT

1. How does the battle of spirit and flesh relate to the prayer of relinquishment?

....

....

....

2. Why is the prayer of relinquishment described as a release to freedom?

....

....

....

3. How does Galatians 2:20, "I have been crucified with Christ and I no longer live, but Christ lives in me. The life I live in the body, I live by faith in the Son of God, who loved me and gave himself for me," fit into the theme of a prayer of relinquishment?

....

....

....

 PARENT PAGE

OBEDIENCE

Andrew Murray put it best: "The starting point and the goal of our Christian life is obedience." If there is a secret to living the Christian life, it is found through obedience. Through our obedient life comes freedom and fulfillment.

Read John 14:21.

1. If we say we love God, what will be the result according to this verse?

....

....

2. Why is this such an important principle in our Christian lives?

....

....

Jesus: The Example of Obedience
Read Philippians 2:5-11.

3. What attitude did Jesus have according to this Scripture?

....

....

4. What was the result of this obedience to Jesus?

....

....

5. What can we do as a family to help one another live a more obedient Christian lifestyle?

....

....

....

Session 2 "The Prayer of Relinquishment" Date..............................

53

DOES GOD ALWAYS ANSWER PRAYER?

KEY VERSE

"**B**ut when you pray, go into your room, close the door and pray to your Father, who is unseen. Then your Father, who sees what is done in secret, will reward you."
Matthew 6:6

BIBLICAL BASIS

Genesis 15:2-5;
Matthew 6:5-7;
Luke 22:42;
Acts 3:1-10;
James 4:2,3

THE BIG IDEA

God always answers prayer in one of three ways: no, go or grow.

AIMS OF THIS SESSION

During this session you will guide students to:
• Examine the various ways God answers prayer;
• Discover prayer principles to use in their relationships with God;
• Implement the prayer principle into their lives in a practical manner.

WARM UP

Prayer Survey—

A survey of stduents' feelings and practice of prayer.

TEAM EFFORT— JUNIOR HIGH/ MIDDLE SCHOOL

God Answers Prayer—
An activity to get students thinking about God answering prayer.

TEAM EFFORT— HIGH SCHOOL

Seventeen-Year-Old Girl Dies—
A news story of an unexpected answer to prayer.

IN THE WORD

Go, No or Grow—
A Bible study on the answers God gives to prayers.

THINGS TO THINK ABOUT (OPTIONAL)

Questions to get students thinking and talking about God answering their prayers.

PARENT PAGE

A tool to get the session into the home and allow parents and young people to discuss accepting God's answers to prayer.

Leader's Devotional

A pastor tells about his wonderful tropical fish aquarium. The man loves those fish, for gazing into their world is a great visual respite for him as he writes. The fish, however, are unaware of his love. When he interacts with the fish, they are terrified of him. They also are prone to illness. When a fish becomes ill, the owner must remove the fish from the tank and medicate it until it is healthy again. This help, necessary to keeping the fish alive, so terrifies the sick fish that the shock can kill it. The author expresses his frustration that there is no way for him to communicate to his fish how much they mean to him, how much time he spends caring for them, how he wants to help them. He, of course, is getting at the point that unless he could become a fish and tell them of his love, they will never know.

We (the fish, so to speak) so often talk about answers to prayer as if we were grading God (our owner and keeper) on His performance. He either did or did not answer our prayer according to what we think He should do! But let's pick up the line of this fish story, if you'll pardon the pun.

The bottom line of our judgmental responses to God's answers usually hinge on our mistrust of Him. That's not a pretty picture for people who sing lustily about faith in God and simply trusting every day. But it's not faith at all to trust Him when He has done what we've asked! Truly trusting Him happens when He doesn't seem to be answering what we view as an urgent need, when He says no to something we are certain we must have. Then true faith stops struggling and folds its hands. It recalls how much He loves us and reaffirms that He really does know what is best for us because His love for us is far greater than even our love for ourselves! He proved His love completely when He came to earth and gave up His life. Paul puts it this way: "He who did not spare his own Son, but gave him up for us all—how will he not also, along with him, graciously give us all things?" (Romans 8:32). There is nothing we want that He won't give to us, if it's what is best for us. Trust Him. He is truly worthy of our trust! (Mary Gross, editor, Gospel Light.)

> **"We should have no doubt that our prayer is acceptable and heard, and we must leave to God the measure, manner, time, and place, for God will surely do what is right."—**
>
> Martin Luther,
> *The Table-Talk of
> Martin Luther* (World
> Publishing, 1952)

DOES GOD ALWAYS ANSWER PRAYER?

KEY VERSE

"But when you pray, go into your room, close the door and pray to your Father, who is unseen. Then your Father, who sees what is done in secret, will reward you." Matthew 6:6

BIBLICAL BASIS

Genesis 15:2-5; Matthew 6:5-7; Luke 22:42; Acts 3:1-10; James 4:2,3

THE BIG IDEA

God always answers prayer in one of three ways: no, go or grow.

WARM UP (5-10 MINUTES)

PRAYER SURVEY

- Give each student a copy of "Prayer Survey" on page 59 and a pen or pencil.

- Students individually complete survey.

Mark an *X* on each line to show your position on the issues presented. There are no correct answers in this survey. The idea is to see just where you stand on the various questions that come up regarding prayer.

1	2	3	4	5	6	7	8	9	10

I believe beyond a shadow of a doubt that God answers prayer. ... I believe there is a God, but I question whether He is personally interested in everything I do.

1	2	3	4	5	6	7	8	9	10

I don't always know how God answers prayers but I always have faith He will. ... When I see an obvious answer I begin to wonder if God answers at all.

---- Fold ----

When we pray asking God for something, He always answers our prayers. Sometimes He says "go." He says "yes" to your request and answers your prayer in the affirmative. Sometimes He says "no." "You asked, but He knows best and simply answers your prayer with a solid "no." "Perhaps, what you have asked for is not best for you. Other times God says "grow." It might be a matter of timing and He wants you to wait on His will. Whether He says "go," "no" or "grow," He is always answering your prayers. Sometimes we think the only time He answers prayer is when He says "yes." That is an improper view of prayer.

When has God answered a prayer of yours with:

Go

No

Grow

Here are three Scriptures that apply to each of the answers to prayer God will give to you. Read each prayer and mark "go," "no" or "grow" for each appropriate Scripture.

Go	No	Grow

Genesis 15:2-5 ....

Luke 22:42 ....

Acts 3:1-10 ....

Role Play One

Act out James 4:2 in a family situation. The family is wealthy and has a 10-year-old child. How does James 4:3 answer the issue in the role play?

Role Play Two

Demonstrate in a pantomime Matthew 6:5-7.

What is the significance of this Scripture to our prayer life?

SO WHAT?

How can you apply these principles from "In the Word" to your own life today?

THINGS TO THINK ABOUT (OPTIONAL)

- Use the questions on page 65 after or as a part of "In the Word."

1. What makes an answer of "no" or "grow" to our prayer so difficult to handle?

2. Why is "no" so often a very good answer to prayer?

3. Where have you seen God's love and care in your life when He gave you an answer you weren't looking for?

PARENT PAGE

- Distribute page to parents.

| I often praise and thank God as well as ask for things. | 1 | 2 | 3 | 4 | 5 | 6 | 7 | 8 | 9 | 10 | I tend to treat God like Santa Claus. Give me this; give me that. |

| When God says "no" I feel it is for my own good. | 1 | 2 | 3 | 4 | 5 | 6 | 7 | 8 | 9 | 10 | It's hard for me to accept a "no" answer. |

| When God answers a prayer, my faith is strengthened. | 1 | 2 | 3 | 4 | 5 | 6 | 7 | 8 | 9 | 10 | Answered prayer is just a coincidence. |

| When God says, "Wait awhile," I accept His timing without reservation. | 1 | 2 | 3 | 4 | 5 | 6 | 7 | 8 | 9 | 10 | I prayed once and God never answered, so I don't pray very much. |

| I find myself praying all during the day. | 1 | 2 | 3 | 4 | 5 | 6 | 7 | 8 | 9 | 10 | Days go by and I never pray. |

| When I don't feel like praying is when I pray the hardest. | 1 | 2 | 3 | 4 | 5 | 6 | 7 | 8 | 9 | 10 | When I don't feel like praying then I don't. |

| I feel as comfortable praying in public as I do alone. | 1 | 2 | 3 | 4 | 5 | 6 | 7 | 8 | 9 | 10 | I don't pray in public. |

| I feel my prayer life is really growing. | 1 | 2 | 3 | 4 | 5 | 6 | 7 | 8 | 9 | 10 | I've almost buried my prayer life. |

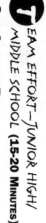

TEAM EFFORT—JUNIOR HIGH/MIDDLE SCHOOL (15-20 MINUTES)

GOD ANSWERS PRAYER

- Have a bag of tricks, such as broken shoelaces and bottle tops, and a bag of treats, such as individually wrapped candies.
- Students sit on the floor in a circle.
- Have students say, "Trick or treat." Give each student a trick or a treat depending upon the position of their legs as they speak to you. If they're sitting with their legs crossed or in

front of their bodies, give a trick. If they're sitting on their legs or have them to one side, give them a treat.
- Ask students: "How did you feel when you received a trick? A treat? Who knows how I decided to give you a trick or a treat? How is this experience like or unlike getting answers to your prayers? Just like we wondered if we were going to get a trick or a treat, we may wonder if God will answer our prayers."
- Again have them each say, "Trick or treat" as you stand in front of them. This time, always give a treat. Afterward say: "It doesn't matter how hard we pray or what we do, God always answers our prayers. We may not receive the answer we expect, but we know God will not ignore or forget us."
- Students perform skit.

TEAM EFFORT—HIGH SCHOOL (15-20 MINUTES)

SEVENTEEN-YEAR-OLD GIRL DIES

- Display a copy of "Seventeen-Year-Old Girl Dies" on page 61 using an overhead projector.
- Read aloud the news story.
- As a whole group, discuss the questions.

A seventeen-year-old girl died after a "faith healer" prayed for her healing and her parents pulled the plug. Against the wishes of the medical staff in the hospital, the parents of 17-year-old Debra Barker stopped her hospital respirator because they believed she was healed. Debra Barker had been in a coma for three days after a tragic accident in which she was thrown from her car. Evidence showed the passengers of the car had been drinking.

Pastor Stephen Johnson of Community Church said that Debra's parents asked Reverend Jesse Thomas, a faith healer who had just preached at the church, to come to the hospital to pray for their daughter. Reverend Thomas, Pastor Johnson and Debra's parents entered the hospital room at approximately 1:00 in the afternoon. After Reverend Thomas prayed for Debra he said she felt warmth flow through his hands onto her forehead. Debra's parents, "in faith," pulled the plug to the respirator without the permission of the hospital staff. Debra died 12 minutes later.

1. Was Reverend Thomas an evil man?

2. Did Debra's parents make a mistake?

3. Where does faith come into the healing process? Since the prayers were sincere, why didn't God heal Debra?

4. What lessons can we learn from this "news story"?

IN THE WORD (25-30 MINUTES)

GO, NO OR GROW

- Divide students into groups of three or four.
- Display a copy of "Go, No or Grow" on pages 63 and 65 using an overhead projector.
- Students complete the Bible study.

WARM UP

PRAYER SURVEY

Mark an *X* on each line to show your position on the issues presented. There are no correct answers in this survey. The idea is to see just where you stand on the various questions that come up regarding prayer.

1	2	3	4	5	6	7	8	9	10

I believe beyond a shadow of a doubt that God answers prayer.

I believe there is a God, but I question whether He is personally interested in everything I do.

1	2	3	4	5	6	7	8	9	10

I don't always know how God answers prayers, but I always have faith He will.

When I see an obvious answer I begin to wonder if God answers at all.

1	2	3	4	5	6	7	8	9	10

I often praise and thank God as well as ask for things.

I tend to treat God like Santa Claus. Give me this; give me that.

1	2	3	4	5	6	7	8	9	10

When God says "no" I feel it is for my own good.

It's hard for me to accept a "no" answer.

1	2	3	4	5	6	7	8	9	10

When God answers a prayer, my faith is strengthened.

Answered prayer is just a coincidence.

1	2	3	4	5	6	7	8	9	10

When God says, "Wait awhile," I accept His timing without reservation.

I prayed once and God never answered, so I don't pray very much.

1	2	3	4	5	6	7	8	9	10

I find myself praying all during the day.

Days go by and I never pray.

1	2	3	4	5	6	7	8	9	10

When I don't feel like praying is when I pray the hardest.

When I don't feel like praying then I don't.

1	2	3	4	5	6	7	8	9	10

I feel as comfortable praying in public as I do alone.

I don't pray in public.

1	2	3	4	5	6	7	8	9	10

I feel my prayer life is really growing.

I've almost buried my prayer life.

TEAM EFFORT

SEVENTEEN-YEAR-OLD GIRL DIES

A seventeen-year-old girl died after a "faith healer" prayed for her healing and her parents pulled the plug. Against the wishes of the medical staff in the hospital, the parents of 17-year-old Debra Barker stopped her hospital respirator because they believed she was healed. Debra Barker had been in a coma for three days after a tragic accident in which she was thrown from her car. Evidence showed the passengers of the car had been drinking.

Pastor Stephen Johnson of Community Church said that Debra's parents asked Reverend Jesse Thomas, a faith healer who had just preached at the church, to come to the hospital to pray for their daughter. Reverend Thomas, Pastor Johnson and Debra's parents entered the hospital room at approximately 1:00 in the afternoon. After Reverend Thomas prayed for Debra he said she was healed as he felt warmth flow through his hands onto her forehead. Debra's parents, "in faith," pulled the plug to the respirator without the permission of the hospital staff. Debra died 12 minutes later.

1. Was Reverend Thomas an evil man?

....

....

....

2. Did Debra's parents make a mistake?

....

....

....

3. Where does faith come into the healing process? Since the prayers were sincere, why didn't God heal Debra?

....

....

....

4. What lessons can we learn from this "news story"?

....

....

....

....

IN THE WORD

GO, NO OR GROW

When we pray asking God for something, He always answers our prayers. Sometimes He says "go." He says "yes" to your request and answers your prayer in the affirmative. Sometimes He says "no." You asked, but He knows best and simply answers your prayer with a solid "no." Perhaps, what you have asked for is not best for you. Other times God says "grow." It might be a matter of timing and He wants you to wait on His will. Whether He says "go," "no" or "grow," He is always answering your prayers. Sometimes we think the only time He answers prayer is when He says "yes." That is an improper view of prayer.

When has God answered a prayer of yours with:

Go...

....

No...

....

Grow...

....

Here are three Scriptures that apply to each of the answers to prayer God will give to you. Read each prayer and mark "go," "no" or "grow" for each appropriate Scripture.

	Go	No	Grow
Genesis 15:2-5			
Luke 22:42			
Acts 3:1-10			

Role Play One

Act out James 4:2 in a family situation. The family is wealthy and has a 10-year-old child.

How does James 4:3 answer the issue in the role play?...

....

Role Play Two

Demonstrate in a pantomime Matthew 6:5-7.

What is the significance of this Scripture to our prayer life?....................................

....

....

....

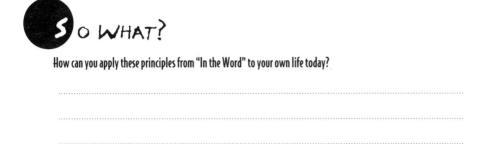

So What?

How can you apply these principles from "In the Word" to your own life today?

....

....

....

Things to Think About

1. What makes an answer of "no" or "grow" to our prayer so difficult to handle?

....

....

....

2. Why is "no" so often a very good answer to prayer?

....

....

....

3. Where have you seen God's love and care in your life when He gave you an answer you weren't looking for?

....

....

....

PARENT PAGE

THE SERENITY PRAYER

Give me the serenity
To accept the things I cannot change;
Give me the courage
To change the things I can, and
The wisdom to distinguish
The one from the other.   FRIEDRICH CHRISTOPH OETINGER

Discussion for the Family

1. What truths do you find in this prayer?

....

....

2. How can we, as a family, use this prayer to make our family stronger? ....

....

....

3. For what do you need serenity? For what do you need courage?

....

....

**4. Pray for the situations just discussed. Then list how as family members you can help and encourage each other
in the situations.** ....

....

....

Session 3 "Does God Always Answer Prayer?" Date ....

67

THE LORD'S PRAYER

KEY VERSES

"This, then, is how you should pray: 'Our Father in heaven, hallowed be your name, your kingdom come, your will be done on earth as it is in heaven. Give us today our daily bread. Forgive us our debts, as we also have forgiven our debtors. And lead us not into temptation, but deliver us from the evil one.'"
Matthew 6:9-13

BIBLICAL BASIS

Matthew 6:9-13

THE BIG IDEA

Jesus used the Lord's Prayer to teach His disciples how to pray. This powerful prayer is very relevant to our spiritual lives today.

AIMS OF THIS SESSION

During this session you will guide students to:

• Examine this most powerful prayer from the lips of Jesus;

• Discover how the Lord's Prayer still relates to their faith today;

• Implement specific ways to apply this prayer to their lives especially in the areas of honoring God, for giving others and overcoming temptation.

WARM UP

Prayer to Me—
A look at students' ideas about prayer.

TEAM EFFORT— JUNIOR HIGH/ MIDDLE SCHOOL

If God Should Speak—
An unexpected dialogue between a young person and God.

TEAM EFFORT— HIGH SCHOOL

Personal Inventory—
An inventory of students' prayer lives.

IN THE WORD

The Model Prayer—
A Bible study on the Lord's Prayer.

THINGS TO THINK ABOUT (OPTIONAL)

Questions to get students thinking and talking about putting the Lord's Prayer into practice.

PARENT PAGE

A tool to get the session into the home and allow parents and young people to discuss priorities in prayer.

LEADER'S DEVOTIONAL

We've heard the homily for years: Prayer changes things. It seems like an innocent idea. There's probably no doubt in our minds that prayer does change things. However, the question is, what "things" *does* prayer change? Is prayer a celestial slot machine, where if we can just get the right combination of words and earnestness, God *will* change His mind and grant us that new Mercedes?! Or instead, might prayer change things we didn't want changed? Prayer is the communion, the passion that makes the most enormous changes known to heaven and earth. But those changes usually come in a different way than we might expect: The changes must come in *us first*! As we learn to pray the kind of prayer Jesus taught, we find that it's more than a pattern for expression. His prayer is a pattern for new attitudes, for reordering our priorities according to the rule of God's kingdom! When we tell God we want His will to be done in our lives the way it is done in heaven, we are pledging a staggering amount of obedience! When we ask that we be forgiven in the way we have forgiven others, we must stop to peel back our layers of righteousness to check for unresolved situations, unforgiven people. This is change, all right! And this kind of change could be dangerous indeed! For Jesus' kind of prayer requires us to let go of our way completely. It requires us to be open to God's Spirit, letting Him change our minds, retake our wills and refocus our thinking. It leads us to readiness to freely lay our dearest hopes and our best ideas on the altar of God's desire for us, willing to slay them if He asks it. When we begin to pray with our hearts as well as our lips, "Your will be done on earth as it is in heaven" (Matthew 6:10), we will find that prayer changes things indeed—by changing us completely.

(Mary Gross, editor, Gospel Light.)

"Every Christian ought to say to the Savior as humbly as [the disciples]: 'Lord, teach us to pray.' Ah! if we were only convinced of our ignorance and of our need of a Teacher like Jesus Christ."—

Jean-Nicholas Grou, *How to Pray* (The Attic Press, 1982)

THE LORD'S PRAYER

KEY VERSES

"This, then, is how you should pray: 'Our Father in heaven, hallowed be your name, your kingdom come, your will be done on earth as it is in heaven. Give us today our daily bread. Forgive us our debts, as we also have forgiven our debtors. And lead us not into temptation, but deliver us from the evil one.'" Matthew 6:9-13

BIBLICAL BASIS

Matthew 6:9-13

THE BIG IDEA

Jesus used the Lord's Prayer to teach His disciples how to pray. This powerful prayer is very relevant to our spiritual lives today.

WARM UP (5-10 MINUTES)

Prayer to Me

• Display a copy of "Prayer to Me" on page 73 using an overhead projector.
• Divide students into groups.
• Students respond to each item and give reasons for their responses.
(complete the statement with one of the choices below and tell your group why you chose that specific one.

	Prayer to me is more	
like		than
☐ a window		☐ a closet
☐ listening		☐ talking
☐ making a friend		☐ seeing an old friend
☐ hard work		☐ time of rest
☐ journey inward		☐ journey outward
☐ discipline		☐ spontaneity

---

on earth as it is in heaven—

Give us today our daily bread—

Forgive us our debts—

as we also have forgiven our debtors—

and lead us not into temptation—

but deliver us from the evil one." –
(Matthew 6:9-13)

SO WHAT?

Now let's take a personal and practical approach to prayer.

1. What are specific ways you can honor God?

2. What can you do to make God's will a bigger part of your life?

3. Is there someone you need to forgive? Write down the names of people you need to forgive and how you will do it.

4. How can you seek God's help in overcoming temptation in your life?

THINGS TO THINK ABOUT (OPTIONAL)

• Use the questions on page 83 after or as a part of "In the Word."
1. How can the Lord's Prayer become nothing more than an everyday ritual?

2. What are ways to keep the Lord's Prayer fresh and important in your spiritual life?

3. According to the Lord's Prayer, why is our forgiveness from the Father conditional on our forgiveness of other people?

PARENT PAGE

• Distribute page to parents.

If God Should Speak

- Assign the skit roles.
- Give each performer a copy of "If God Should Speak" on pages 75 and 77. If possible, do this before the session so performers have an opportunity to rehearse.
- Student playing the part of God should be offstage and out of sight. Students perform skit.
- Introduce the skit to the audience by saying, "Prayer is a dangerous thing. You could wind up with some major changes in your life."

TEAM EFFORT—HIGH SCHOOL (15-20 MINUTES)

Personal Inventory

- Give each student a copy of "Personal Inventory" on page 79 and a pen or pencil.
- Students complete the page individually.
- As a whole group, discuss students' responses.

1. **Adoration**—"Our Father in heaven, hallowed be your name." I spend time praising God for who He is—the sovereign Lord and ruler of the universe who cares about me personally, as though I am the only person in the world.

I'm Weak Here	I'm Strong Here

2. **Intercession**—"Your kingdom come, your will be done on earth as it is in heaven." I spend time praying about the needs of the world. I try to look at the world the way God looks at it and pray about the things that are on the heart of God.

I'm Weak Here	I'm Strong Here

3. **Asking**—"Give us today our daily bread." When I ask for myself, I ask simply for the necessities of life—food, shelter and contentment—mindful that there are so many in the world without these.

I'm Weak Here	I'm Strong Here

4. **Forgiveness**—"Forgive us our debts, as we also have forgiven our debtors." In my prayer time, I consciously recall the relationships in my family and with my associates where I have been hurt or hurt others and ask for forgiveness.

I'm Weak Here	I'm Strong Here

---

5. **Temptation**—"And lead us not into temptation, but deliver us from the evil one." In my prayer time, I allow God to speak to me about the areas where I am struggling or treading on dangerous ground.

I'm Weak Here	I'm Strong Here

IN THE WORD (25-30 MINUTES)

The Model Prayer

- Divide students into groups of three or four.
- Give each student a copy of "The Model Prayer" on pages 81 and 83 and a pen or pencil.
- Students complete the Bible study.

The most famous prayer in the Scriptures is what we often call the Lord's Prayer. Many Christian denominations repeat this prayer every week in their services. The beauty, intensity and significance of this prayer of Jesus is unequaled in Scripture. Jesus was teaching His disciples how to pray and He told them to use this prayer as an example.
Looking at the Scripture: Read Matthew 6:9-13.

What is significant about the way Jesus addressed the Father?
(Jesus calls God "Father" which was very unusual.)

How did Jesus place His life in the will of the Father?
(Jesus gave up His own will to do the work of the Father.)

What concerns does Jesus pray about in the prayer?
(For God's kingdom to be established, for His will to be done, for His and other's physical needs to be met, for forgiveness and to be kept from temptation and evil)

In your own words, write each line of the Lord's Prayer:

"Our Father in heaven—

....

hallowed be your name—

....

your kingdom come—

....

your will be done—

....

Fold

WARM UP

PRAYER TO ME[1]

Complete the statement with one of the choices below and tell your group why you chose
that specific one.

Prayer to me is more

like	than
☐ a window	a closet ☐
☐ listening	talking ☐
☐ making a friend	seeing an old friend ☐
☐ hard work	time of rest ☐
☐ journey inward	journey outward ☐
☐ discipline	spontaneity ☐

Note

1. Adapted from *The Serendipity Bible Study Book* (Grand Rapids, MI: Zondervan, 1986), p. 33.
   Used by permission.

 **T**EAM **E**FFORT

I**F** G**OD** S**HOULD** S**PEAK**[1]

Student: "Our Father which art in heaven..."

God: Yes.

Student: Don't interrupt me. I'm praying.

God: But you called Me.

Student: Called You? I didn't call You. I'm praying. "Our Father which art in heaven..."

God: There, you did it again.

Student: Did what?

God: Called Me. You said, "Our Father which art in heaven." Here I am. What's on your mind?

Student: But I didn't mean anything by it. I was, you know, just saying my prayers for the day. I always say the Lord's Prayer. It makes me feel good, kind of like getting a duty done.

God: All right. Go on!

Student: "Hallowed be thy name..."

God: Hold it! What do you mean by that?

Student: By what?

God: By "Hallowed be thy name?"

Student: It means...it means...good grief! I don't know what it means! How should I know? It's just part of the prayer. By the way, what does it mean?

God: It means honored, holy, wonderful.

Student: Hey that makes sense. I never thought what hallowed meant before. "Thy kingdom come, thy will be done, on earth as it is in heaven."

God: Do you really mean that?

Student: Sure, why not?

God: What are you doing about it?

Student: Doing? Nothing, I guess. I just think it would be kind of neat if You got control of everything down here like You have up there.

God: Have I got control of you?

Student: Well, I go to church.

God: That isn't what I asked you. What about that habit of lying you have? And your temper? You've really got a problem there, you know. And then there's the way you spend your money...all on yourself. And what about the kind of books you read?

Student: Stop picking on me! I'm just as good as some of the rest of those people—those phonies—at church!

God: Excuse me! I thought you were praying for My will to be done. If that is to happen, it will have to start with the ones who are praying for it. Like you, for example.

Student: Oh, all right. I guess. I do have some problems, some hang-ups. Now that You mention it, I could probably name some others.

God: So could I.

Student: I haven't thought about it very much until now, but I really would like to cut out some of those things. I would like to, you know, be really free.

God: Good! Now we are getting somewhere. We'll work together, you and I. Some victories can truly be won; I'm proud of you!

Student: Look, Lord! I need to finish up here. This is taking a lot longer than it usually does. "Give us this day, our daily bread."

God: You need to cut out some of that "bread." You're overweight as it is.

Student: Hey, wait a minute! What is this, "Criticize Me Day"? Here I was doing my religious duty, and all of a sudden You break in and remind me of all my problems and shortcomings.

God: Prayer is a dangerous thing. You could wind up changed, you know. That's what I'm trying to get across to you. You called me, and here I am. It's too late to stop now. Keep on praying. I'm interested in the next part of your prayer... (Pause.) Well go on!

Student: I'm afraid to.

God: Afraid? Afraid of what?

Student: I know what You'll say next.

God: Try Me and see.

Student: "Forgive us our trespasses, as we forgive those who trespass against us."

God: What about Joe?

Student: I knew it! See, I knew You would bring him up! Why, Lord, he's told lies about me, and cheated me out of some money, and he is the biggest phony around. He never paid back that debt he owes me. I've sworn to get even with him and then never associate with him again!

God: But your prayer! What about your prayer?

Student: I didn't mean it.

God: Well, at least you're honest. But it's not much fun carrying that load of bitterness around inside you, is it?

Student: No, but I'll feel better as soon as I get even. Boy, have I got some plans for old Joe! He'll wish he never did me any harm.

God: You won't feel any better. You'll only feel worse. Revenge isn't sweet. Think of how unhappy you are already. But I can change all that.

Student: You can? How?

God: Forgive Joe. Then the hate and sin will be Joe's problem, not yours. You may lose the money, but you will have settled your heart.

Student: But Lord, I can't forgive Joe.

God: Then how do you expect Me to forgive you?

Student: Oh, You're right! You always are! And more than I want revenge on Joe, I need to be right with You. All right, I forgive him Lord, You help him to find the right road in life. He's bound to be awfully miserable now that I think about it. Anybody who goes around doing some of the things he does to others has to be out of it. Someway, some how, show him the right way. Maybe You can even help me to help him?

God: There now! Wonderful! How do you feel?

Student: Hmmm! Well, not bad. Not bad at all. In fact, I feel pretty great! You know, I don't think I'll have to go to bed uptight tonight for the first time since I can remember. Maybe I won't be so tired from now on because I'm not getting enough rest.

God: You're not through with your prayer. Go on!

Student: Oh, all right. "And lead us not into temptation, but deliver us from evil."

God: Good! Good! I'll do that. Just don't put yourself in a place where you can be tempted.

Student: What do You mean by that?

God: Change some of your friendships. Some of your so-called friends are beginning to get to you. Don't be fooled! They advertise that they're having fun, but for you it could be ruin. Either you are going to have to stop being with them, or start being a positive influence on their lives. Don't You use Me as an escape hatch!

Student: I don't understand.

God: Sure you do. You've done it a lot of times. You get caught in a bad situation. You get into trouble by not listening to Me, and then once you do, you come running to Me saying, "Lord, God: Sure you do. You've done it a lot of times. You get caught in a bad situation. You get into trouble by not listening to Me, and then once you do, you come running to Me saying, "Lord, help me out of this mess, and I promise You I'll never do it again." You remember some of those bargains you tried to make with Me, don't you?

Student: Yes, I do, and I'm ashamed, Lord. I really am.

God: Which bargain are you remembering?

Student: Well, when the woman next door saw me coming out of that X-rated movie with my friends. I'd told my mother we were going to the mall. I remember telling You, "Oh, God don't let her tell my mother where I've been." I promised to be in church every Sunday.

God: She didn't tell your mother, but you didn't keep your promise, did you?

Student: I'm sorry, Lord, I really am. Up until now, I thought that if I just prayed the Lord's Prayer every day then I could do what I liked. I didn't expect anything like this to happen.

God: Go ahead and finish your prayer!

Student: "For thine is the kingdom, and the power, and the glory, for ever. Amen."

God: Do you know what would bring Me glory? What would make Me really happy?

Student: No, but I'd like to know. I want to please You. I know what a difference it can make in my life. I can see what a mess I've made of my life, and I can see how great it would be to really be one of Your followers.

God: You just answered my question.

Student: I did?

God: Yes. The thing that would bring Me glory is to have people like you truly love Me. And I see that happening between us now. Now that these old sins are exposed and out of the way, well, there's no telling what we can do together.

Student: Lord, let's see what we can make of me and my life, OK?

God: Yes, let's see!

Note

1. Adapted from Walt Kukkonen, "If God Should Speak," *Ideas* 23 (El Cajon, CA: Youth Specialties, 1980), pp. 35-39. Used by permission.

*T*EAM *E*FFORT

*P*ERSONAL *I*NVENTORY[1]

1. Adoration—"Our Father in heaven, hallowed be your name." I spend time praising God for who He is—the sovereign Lord and ruler of the universe who cares about me personally, as though I am the only person in the world.

I'm Weak Here   I'm Strong Here

2. Intercession—"Your kingdom come, your will be done on earth as it is in heaven." I spend time praying about the needs of the world. I try to look at the world the way God looks at it and pray about the things that are on the heart of God.

I'm Weak Here   I'm Strong Here

3. Asking—"Give us today our daily bread." When I ask for myself, I ask simply for the necessities of life—food, shelter and contentment—mindful that there are so many in the world without these.

I'm Weak Here   I'm Strong Here

4. Forgiveness—"Forgive us our debts, as we also have forgiven our debtors." In my prayer time, I consciously recall the relationships in my family and with my associates where I have been hurt or hurt others and ask for forgiveness.

I'm Weak Here   I'm Strong Here

5. Temptation—"And lead us not into temptation, but deliver us from the evil one." In my prayer time, I allow God to speak to me about the areas where I am struggling or treading on dangerous ground.

I'm Weak Here   I'm Strong Here

Note

1. Adapted from *The Serendipity Bible Study Book* (Grand Rapids, MI: Zondervan, 1986), p. 33. Used by permission.

IN THE WORD

THE MODEL PRAYER

The most famous prayer in the Scriptures is what we often call the Lord's Prayer. Many Christian denominations repeat this prayer every week in their services. The beauty, intensity and significance of this prayer of Jesus is unequaled in Scripture. Jesus was teaching His disciples how to pray and He told them to use this prayer as an example.

Looking at the Scripture: Read Matthew 6:9-13.

What is significant about the way Jesus addressed the Father?

....

How did Jesus place His life in the will of the Father?

....

What concerns does Jesus pray about in the prayer?

....

In your own words, write each line of the Lord's Prayer:

"Our Father in heaven—

....

hallowed be your name—

....

your kingdom come—

....

your will be done—

....

on earth as it is in heaven—

....

Give us today our daily bread—

....

Forgive us our debts—

....

as we also have forgiven our debtors—

....

and lead us not into temptation—

....

but deliver us from the evil one."—

....

(Matthew 6:9-13)

*S*O WHAT?

Now let's take a personal and practical approach to prayer.

1. What are specific ways you can honor God?

....

....

2. What can you do to make God's will a bigger part of your life?

....

....

3. Is there someone you need to forgive? Write down the names of people you need to forgive and how you will do it.

....

....

4. How can you seek God's help in overcoming temptation in your life?

....

....

*T*HINGS TO THINK ABOUT

1. How can the Lord's Prayer become nothing more than an everyday ritual?

....

....

2. What are ways to keep the Lord's Prayer fresh and important in your spiritual life?

....

....

3. According to the Lord's Prayer, why is our forgiveness from the Father conditional on our forgiveness of other people?

....

....

....

PARENT PAGE

Our Father in heaven, hallowed be your name, your kingdom come, your will be done on earth as it is in heaven. Give us today our daily bread. Forgive us our debts, as we also have forgiven our debtors. And lead us not into temptation, but deliver us from the evil one (Matthew 6:9-13).

Take a few moments to look at the Lord's Prayer and then use the space below to list important attitudes, requests and priorities you discover in the prayer.

Attitudes:...

Requests:...

Priorities:...

The Lord's Prayer is actually about priorities. It's so easy to let the truly important issues of life get out of focus. If you are like most of us, you tend to put off dealing with the most significant priorities and spend most of your time on the less important, minor issues of life.

Take a few moments to write down your life priorities in the order you believe would most glorify God.

1...

2...

3...

4...

5...

6...

7...

8...

9...

10..

Session 4 "The Lord's Prayer" Date...............................

DEVELOPING A DISCIPLINED DEVOTIONAL LIFE

LEADER'S PEP TALK

I've told students for years that a disciplined devotional life with God was not an option but a necessity for spiritual growth. However, for most of my years of youth ministry it has been one of the greatest struggles of my life. I have tried every "devotional program" ever written and failed miserably at all of them. I think I kept waiting for "the feeling," whatever that means.

Then one day in the quietness of my bedroom I got on my knees before God and I said something like, "Lord, I'm ashamed of what little time I spend with you." I almost expected a lightening bolt to come out of heaven and zap me. Out of my lack of discipline and my desire to grow in my relationship with God I started to say, "Lord, I will commit two hours a day of devotional time with you."

A friend of mine in seminary told me Billy Graham gave God a tenth of his day. However, I knew that wouldn't last so I started to say, "God, I will give you one hour everyday for the rest of my life." If my friend Becky can do that then I surely can do the same. Again, I knew I was opting for failure. Half hour, "nope." "Okay, God, I'll give you 20 minutes a day for the rest of my life." I half expected a "what a spiritual wimp" to come from the voice of God, but rather I sensed a real peace.

That commitment was in 1985. I've missed a few days, but not many. I can't always remember what I read or prayed about, but then I can't tell you what I ate last week, although the food nourishes me today.

Paul's advice to Timothy was "train yourself to be godly" (1 Timothy 4:7). Our job in this section is not to pour heaps of guilt and try to shame our students into a devotional life. We know in our heart that that won't work. However, our goal is to give our students every opportunity to listen to the Word of God and practically develop a devotional life that works for them.

Christian psychologists tell us that it only takes three weeks to form a habit and another three weeks to solidify that habit for life. We tend to talk in church about bad habits more often than good habits. Yet developing a daily time with God is a *great* habit. You have the privilege in these next few sessions to provide an "apple of gold" for your students. As you guide them into developing a regular time of communication and

devotion to God, you will help your young people change their spiritual lives *forever*. (Who says youth work isn't important!)

Here's the theme for this section of the curriculum:

"Do not let this Book of the Law depart from your mouth; meditate on it day and night, so that you may be careful to do everything written in it. Then you will be prosperous and successful" (Joshua 1:8).

Caution: These next few sessions may cause an eternal difference in the lives of your students. Thanks again for your availability to be a difference-maker in the lives of your students. God bless you!

DEVELOPING A DISCIPLINED DEVOTIONAL LIFE

KEY VERSE

"Very early in the morning, while it was still dark, Jesus got up, left the house and went off to a solitary place, where he prayed."
Mark 1:35

BIBLICAL BASIS

Joshua 1:8;
Psalm 150:6;
Proverbs 2:1,2,5;
Matthew 7:7;
Mark 1:35;
1 Thessalonians 5:18;
1 Timothy 4:7;
1 Peter 1:24,25;
1 John 1:9

THE BIG IDEA

Developing a disciplined devotional life is not an option but a necessity for spiritual growth.

AIMS OF THIS SESSION

During this session you will guide students to:
- Examine the importance of a disciplined devotional life;
- Discover the elements of a devotional life;
- Implement a specific, regular daily devotional in their own lives.

WARM UP

Your Choice—
An opportunity for young people to share.

TEAM EFFORT— JUNIOR HIGH/ MIDDLE SCHOOL

A Devotional Life Inventory—
An inventory of students' time with God.

TEAM EFFORT— HIGH SCHOOL

A Letter from God—
A look at God's desire to spend time with His children.

IN THE WORD

A Letter from God—
A Bible study on the elements of a devotional life.

THINGS TO THINK ABOUT (OPTIONAL)

Questions to get students thinking and talking about their devotional lives.

PARENT PAGE

A tool to get the session into the home and allow parents and young people to discuss spending time with God.

LEADER'S DEVOTIONAL

There once was a boy who lived in his father's home where his dad took care to provide him with everything he needed. The father also gave his son many other things, just to show his love.

But the boy seldom returned his father's displays of affection. He rarely talked to his father at all, for there were so many other things to do, so many other ways to spend his time other than with his dad. He accepted his dad's gifts; sometimes when he used them, he offered a brief "Thank you" in passing. But time spent in building a relationship with dad wasn't a priority.

The boy really didn't know his father as a person. Dad was just the provider of resources. He had to admit he really didn't know what his dad was like—what made him happy or what things he cared about. In a sense, he was his father's son in name only.

Does this sound like your average "ungrateful child"? Or really, does it sound more like you and me? Yes, we are related to our Father and are living in His house of grace. He goes above and beyond the call of duty to prove His love for us. He constantly calls our names, makes efforts to bring us close to Him. But are we His children in name only?

Until we carve out time and make regular opportunities to get to know our Father for who He is, to begin to appreciate Him for Himself, we remain at the level of self-absorbed children who are His in name only. It's not enough to be passingly thankful for the gifts but rarely stopping to get intimate with the Giver. And as we have already seen, intimacy with God is what changes us and grows us into people who *know* Him, not people who know *about* Him. He is not looking for a legalistic, hours-long commitment to some religious form: He wants *you*. And there is no sweeter, more valuable time in life this side of heaven—no matter what the tyranny of the urgent seems to be screaming at us.

Crises will always be there. But to give God the best of ourselves in a new day, to spend time talking with Him at night, is a discipline that will soon grow to a hunger for His presence, if we will lay down our preconceived notions of what we have to *do* and let our Father guide us into intimate relationship with Him. Grow beyond being His child in name only! (Mary Gross, editor, Gospel Light.)

"A spiritual life without discipline is impossible. Discipline is the other side of discipleship."—

Henri Nouwen, *Making All Things New*, (Harper & Row, 1981)

DEVELOPING A DISCIPLINED DEVOTIONAL LIFE

K EY VERSE

"Very early in the morning, while it was still dark, Jesus got up, left the house and went off to a solitary place, where he prayed." Mark 1:35

B IBLICAL BASIS

Joshua 1:8; Psalm 150:6; Proverbs 2:1,2,5; Matthew 7:7; Mark 1:35; 1 Thessalonians 5:18; 1 Timothy 4:7; 1 Peter 1:24,25; 1 John 1:9

T HE BIG IDEA

Developing a disciplined devotional life is not an option but a necessity for spiritual growth.

W ARM UP (5-10 MINUTES)

YOUR CHOICE

- Display a copy of "Your Choice" on page 93 using an overhead projector.
- Divide students into groups of three or four.
- Students discuss questions.

1. If you could develop any talent what would it be? Why?

2. If you had to choose between getting up early to help build a parade float or sleeping in on Saturday morning which would you choose? Why?

3. Which phrase best describes you?
.... Totally disciplined to the point of boring.
.... More disciplined than most.
.... Sometimes disciplined, other times not.
.... Spontaneous at all times.
.... Flake.

------------------------------ Fold ------------------------------

S O WHAT?

Now that you have had a devotional time as part of this session, what keeps you from doing it on a daily basis? Fill in this section individually.

An Appointment with God

A specific time to meet with God ....

Amount of time to meet with God ....

A quiet place to meet with God ....

Some specific methods for my time with God ....

T HINGS TO THINK ABOUT (OPTIONAL)

- Use the questions on page 101 after or as a part of "In the Word."

1. Why is it difficult for most people to have a consistent time with God?

2. Name at least three ways a disciplined quiet time can bring you closer to God.

3. When is the best time of the day for you to take a few moments to be with the Lord?

4. How can you integrate your own creativity into your times with God?

P ARENT PAGE

- Distribute page to parents.

TEAM EFFORT—JUNIOR HIGH/MIDDLE SCHOOL (15-20 MINUTES)

A DEVOTIONAL LIFE INVENTORY
- Give each student a copy of "A Devotional Life Inventory" on page 95 and a pen or pencil.
- Students individually complete pages.
- As a whole group, discuss students' responses.

A disciplined daily devotional life is not an option for spiritual growth; it's a must! For you to grow spiritually you will need to pray daily, read your Bible daily and fellowship with other Christians regularly.

How would you rate your devotional life right now?
___ Hoping to get started.
___ Up and down.
___ Boring.
___ Getting better.
___ Going strong.
___ What devotional life?
___ Really hard to remain disciplined.
___ Other

What would it take for you to improve in this area of your life?

TEAM EFFORT—HIGH SCHOOL (15-20 MINUTES)

A LETTER FROM GOD
- Give each student a copy of "A Letter from God" on page 97 and a pen or pencil.
- Students individually complete pages.
- As a whole group, discuss students' responses.

Imagine walking up to your mailbox and finding an envelope addressed to you and all the return address said was: God. Here's what's inside.

My Dear Child,
I love you. I desire to spend as much time with you as possible. I took great joy in being part of your creation and your salvation. I consider My sacrifice for you a sign of My significant love for you. My child, I want the best for you. I believe in you. I look forward to our daily times together. It gives Me great pleasure to spend time with you. Don't forget, I'm always with you.
Love,
God

1. How would you feel?

2. What decisions would you want to make about your time with God? You can estimate that the average person spends over two hours a day watching television, two hours a day listening to music, two hour a day dressing and grooming, and one hour a day eating. And yet the majority of people spend little or no time each day with God.

3. A wise pastor once asked, "What is so important that you can't spend 15 minutes a day with God?" What's your answer?

4. What makes it so difficult to set up a regular daily time with God?

IN THE WORD (25-30 MINUTES)

ELEMENTS OF AN EFFECTIVE DEVOTIONAL LIFE
- Divide students into groups of three or four.
- Give each student a copy of "Elements of an Effective Devotional Life" on pages 99 and 101 and a pen or pencil.
- Students complete the Bible study.

Read the six elements of an effective devotional life and then enjoy some time with God.

Bible reading
For, "All men are like grass, and all their glory is like the flowers of the field; the grass withers and the flowers fall, but the word of the Lord stands forever." And this is the word that was preached to you (1 Peter 1:24,25).

Listening
My son, if you accept my words and store up my commands within you, turning your ear to wisdom and applying your heart to understanding, then you will understand the fear of the Lord and find the knowledge of God (Proverbs 2:1,2,5).

ACTS
Adoration
Let everything that has breath praise the Lord. Praise the Lord (Psalm 150:6).

Confession
If we confess our sins, he is faithful and just and will forgive us our sins and purify us from all unrighteousness (1 John 1:9).

Thanksgiving
Give thanks in all circumstances, for this is God's will for you in Christ Jesus (1 Thessalonians 5:18).

Supplication (asking)
Ask and it will be given to you; seek and you will find; knock and the door will be opened to you (Matthew 7:7).

Now as a group have a personal time of prayer. Listen for the Holy Spirit to speak in a still, small voice:
1. Read one or two of your favorite Scriptures.
2. Listen silently to the Lord during a time of reflection with God. Take the next 10 minutes to: or impression.
3. Adoration—Take two minutes to tell God of His greatness and His majestic power. Adore Him for who He is: the Lord of lords and the King of kings.
4. Confession—We keep the communication lines open when we confess our sins to God. Take one minute to sit quietly before the Lord. Individually and silently, confess your sins to God. Don't forget to thank Him for His forgiveness.
5. Thanksgiving—As a group, practice thank therapy by going around the group and thanking God for specific ways He has worked in your lives.
6. Supplication (asking)—Now take two to five minutes and ask God for specific prayer requests. Pray for your family, church, school, friends, the government and yourself.

WARM UP

YOUR CHOICE

1. If you could develop any talent what would it be? Why?

....

....

....

2. If you had to choose between getting up early to help build a parade float or sleeping in on Saturday morning which would you choose? Why?

....

....

3. Which phrase best describes you?

.............Totally disciplined to the point of boring

.............More disciplined than most

.............Sometimes disciplined, other times not

.............Spontaneous at all times

.............Flake

TEAM EFFORT

A DEVOTIONAL LIFE INVENTORY

A disciplined daily devotional life is not an option for spiritual growth; it's a must! For you to grow spiritually you will need to pray daily, read your Bible daily and fellowship with other Christians regularly.

How would you rate your devotional life right now?

.... Hoping to get started.

.... Up and down.

.... Boring.

.... Getting better.

.... Going strong.

.... What devotional life?

.... Really hard to remain disciplined.

.... Other..

What would it take for you to improve in this area of your life?

....

....

....

TEAM EFFORT

A LETTER FROM GOD

Imagine walking up to your mailbox and finding an envelope addressed to you and all the return address said was: God.

Here's what's inside.

My Dear Child,

I love you. I desire to spend as much time with you as possible. I took great joy in being part of your creation and your salvation. I consider My sacrifice for you a sign of My significant love for you. My child, I want the best for you. I believe in you. I look forward to our daily times together. It gives Me great pleasure to spend time with you. Don't forget, I'm always with you.

Love,
God

1. How would you feel?

....

....

....

2. What decisions would you want to make about your time with God?

....

....

You can estimate that the average person spends *over* two hours a day watching television, two hours a day listening to music, one hour a day dressing and grooming, and one hour a day eating. And yet the majority of people spend little or no time each day with God.

3. A wise pastor once asked, "What is so important that you can't spend 15 minutes a day with God?" What's your answer?

....

....

....

4. What makes it so difficult to set up a regular daily time with God?

....

....

....

IN THE WORD

ELEMENTS OF AN EFFECTIVE DEVOTIONAL LIFE

Read the six elements of an effective devotional life and then enjoy some time with God.

Bible reading

> For, "All men are like grass, and all their glory is like the flowers of the field; the grass withers and the flowers fall, but the word of the Lord stands forever," And this is the word that was preached to you (1 Peter 1:24,25).

Listening

> My son, if you accept my words and store up my commands within you, turning your ear to wisdom and applying your heart to understanding, then you will understand the fear of the LORD and find the knowledge of God (Proverbs 2:1,2,5).

ACTS
Adoration

> Let everything that has breath praise the LORD. Praise the LORD (Psalm 150:6).

Confession

> If we confess ours sins, he is faithful and just and will forgive us our sins and purify us from all unrighteousness (1 John 1:9).

Thanksgiving

> Give thanks in all circumstances, for this is God's will for you in Christ Jesus (1 Thessalonians 5:18).

Supplication (asking)

> Ask and it will be given to you; seek and you will find; knock and the door will be opened to you (Matthew 7:7).

Now as a group have a personal time of reflection with God. Take the next 10 minutes to:

1. Read one or two or your favorite Scriptures.
2. Listen silently to the Lord during a time of prayer. Listen for the Holy Spirit to speak in a still, small voice or impression.
3. Adoration—Take two minutes to tell God of His greatness and His majestic power. Adore Him for who He is: the Lord of lords and the King of kings.
4. Confession—We keep the communication lines open when we confess our sins to God. Take one minute to sit quietly before the Lord. Individually and silently, confess your sins to God. Don't forget to thank Him for His forgiveness.
5. Thanksgiving—As a group, practice thank therapy by going around the group and thanking God for specific ways He has worked in your lives.
6. Supplication (asking)—Now take two to five minutes and ask God for specific prayer requests. Pray for your family, church, school, friends, the government and yourself.

O WHAT?

Now that you have had a devotional time as part of this session, what keeps you from doing it on a daily basis?
Fill in this section individually.

An Appointment with God

A specific time to meet with God...

Amount of time to meet with God..

A quiet place to meet with God..

Some specific methods for my time with God...

....

THINGS TO THINK ABOUT

1. Why is it difficult for most people to have a consistent time with God?

....

....

....

2. Name at least three ways a disciplined quiet time can bring you closer to God.

....

....

....

3. When is the best time of the day for you to take a few moments to be with the Lord?

....

....

....

4. How can you integrate your own creativity into your times with God?

....

....

 ## Parent Page

Three Scriptures to look at on: Developing a Disciplined Devotional Life

Train yourself to be godly (1 Timothy 4:7).

1. How does discipline and godliness walk hand in hand?

....

Very early in the morning, while it was still dark, Jesus got up, left the house and

went off to a solitary place, where he prayed (Mark 1:35).

2. First read Mark 1:29-34. Jesus experienced busy hectic days just like us! Why did Jesus need to find a quiet place to be with God?

....

Do not let this Book of the Law depart from your mouth; meditate on it day and

night, so that you may be careful to do everything written in it (Joshua 1:8).

3. Summarize this verse.

....

4. What is the formula for a prosperous and successful life? (Notice that prosperity does not necessarily mean financial wealth. It is much closer to meaning a fulfilled and abundant life.)

....

5. What are ways that we as a family can develop a stronger spiritual life together and also help each other with our individual time with God?

....

....

Session 5 "Developing a Disciplined Devotional Life" Date ....

WORSHIP

KEY VERSE

"**C**ome, let us bow down in worship, let us kneel before the LORD our Maker." Psalm 95:6

BIBLICAL BASIS

Psalm 95:6; 100, 122; **J**ohn 14:27

THE BIG IDEA

Worship is an important but often misunderstood part of communication with God.

AIMS OF THIS SESSION

During this session you will guide students to:

• Examine how worship applies to a relationship with God;
• Discover the elements of worship and how they relate to their relationships with God;
• Implement a proper understanding of worship in worship services and in their own personal lives.

WARM UP

Twenty Most Often Used Excuses for Not Coming to Church—
Students brainstorm why people don't come to church.

TEAM EFFORT— **J**UNIOR HIGH/ **M**IDDLE SCHOOL

Worship Association—
A word association of a worship service.

TEAM EFFORT— **H**IGH SCHOOL

Creative Worship—
Students plan their own worship service.

IN THE WORD

The Pursuit of Worship—
A Bible study on attitudes and actions in worship.

THINGS TO THINK **A**BOUT (OPTIONAL)

Questions to get students thinking and talking about worshiping God.

PARENT PAGE

A tool to get the session into the home and allow parents and young people to discuss their levels of participation in worship.

LEADER'S DEVOTIONAL

What image does "worship" call into your mind? Tall stained-glass windows, organ music, choirs robed and harmonious? Or is it the majesty of a quiet, distant mountain cathedral, the glory of a beautiful forest? Where do you worship?

Perhaps it's easier to give priority to worship's place and form than it is to understand worshiping in spirit and truth. But inside we know that worshiping is not a place. Nor is worship about form or about ways to express our love to God. It's not only about church meetings, even though it's wonderful to worship as a family with our brothers and sisters. Because even in church, there can only be corporate worship at the level of what the individual worshipers bring. If we aren't worshiping God every day, we have nothing to bring with which to worship when the Body meets!

So what is worship? It is, as Jesus said, a matter of spirit and truth. It's what is going on in your heart *before* anything reaches your lips. First, it's that daily time to stop and *appreciate* God, time taken both in a block, where we focus on Him, and in little moments, where we pause to give Him the honor and reverence that is His due. It's being *with* Him, in awareness and attention, talking to Him, listening to Him and telling ourselves (and whoever else is listening) that God alone is worthy of all our praise. Worship can happen on a city street or even in the humble bathroom. It's not place; it's not form. It's a spirit full of praise and a mind growing in the truth of God's Word. It's the sacrifice we are required to make (see Hebrews 13:15), the sacrifice that is delightful to bring to the One who is so very worthy of our worship! (Mary Gross, editor, Gospel Light.)

"You are the Fountain of Life, the Treasure of everlasting goods to whom the heavens sing praise—all the angels and heavenly powers, crying out to one another—while we, the weak and unworthy join with them in singing: 'Holy, holy, holy, Lord of God of Hosts, the whole earth is full of your glory.'"—

Lancelot Andrews,
Lancelot Andrews and His Private Devotions
(Baker, 1981)

WORSHIP

KEY VERSE
"Come, let us bow down in worship, let us kneel before the LORD our Maker." Psalm 95:6

BIBLICAL BASIS
Psalm 95:6; 100; 122; John 14:27

THE BIG IDEA
Worship is an important but often misunderstood part of communication with God.

WARM UP (5-10 MINUTES)

TWENTY MOST OFTEN USED EXCUSES FOR NOT COMING TO CHURCH
- Have available a chalkboard and chalk or an overhead projector and pens.
- Have students brainstorm the 20 most often used excuses for not coming to church. (For example, "I had too late a night last night"; "It's my only morning to sleep in"; The girls/guys at church aren't cute enough.")
- Have students vote for: the most ridiculous, most often used, makes most sense, would hurt God's feelings, would make God laugh and the least understood. You can choose others as well.

TEAM EFFORT—JUNIOR HIGH/ MIDDLE SCHOOL (15-20 MINUTES)

WORSHIP ASSOCIATION
- Give each student a piece of paper and a pen or pencil.
- Read the following words and have students quickly list any thoughts that come to their minds. Remind them to not stop to analyze these thoughts now, just jot them down: worship, church, sermon, sacraments, offering, prayer, time with God and worship music.
- Have students share why they responded as they did. Then discuss how your group could change in these areas.

Fold

TEAM EFFORT—HIGH SCHOOL (15-20 MINUTES)

CREATIVE WORSHIP

- Have available a chalkboard and chalk or an overhead projector and pens.
- Have students brainstorm creative ways to have a worship service. Develop an order of service, the desired elements and a plan for carrying it out. Then set a date to have the worship service.

IN THE WORD (25-30 MINUTES)

THE PURSUIT OF WORSHIP

- Divide students into groups of three or four.
- Give each student a copy of "The Pursuit of Worship" on pages 109, 111 and 113 and a pen or pencil.
- Students complete the Bible study.

Worship—the honor and reverence paid to God

1. **Give God your attitude.**

   a. Give God your attitude.

      (Full of excitement and joy.)

   b. **Read Psalm 122. What is the attitude of the person speaking in verse 1?**

   c. A great philosopher once said, "When it comes to worship we should never ask 'How did I do?' We should ask 'How was it?'" How is this statement different from what most people think of when it comes to worship?

      (Most people are looking to receive something, not give something.)

   d. **To participate and enjoy a good worship experience we must develop a proper attitude toward worship. How do you prepare for your worship experience?**

2. **Give God your praise.**

   a. **According to Psalm 122:3,4, why did the tribes of the Lord come to Jerusalem?**

      (To praise God according to His statute.)

   b. **Read Psalm 100. How did you read the verses?**

   c. **What specific things can you do to understand and enjoy your worship experience? Start your next worship experience with a new attitude.**

   d. **What relationship do you find between worship and praise?**

      (Worship and praise go hand in hand. To adore God is to also revere and honor Him.)

3. **Give God your prayers.**

   a. **According to Psalm 122:6-8, what did the writer of this psalm pray for?**

      (Peace for Jerusalem and God's people.)

   b. **How is time spent with God in prayer a form of worship?**

      (In prayer we declare who God is and give Him honor.)

   c. **Reread verses 6-8. The setting is at least 2,500 years ago in Israel. How could you modernize these prayers and make them pertinent to your life today?**

      (Pray for the peace of our city, state, nation and the world. Pray for peace for our brothers and sisters in Christ.)

Fold

4. **The Product of Worship**

   Peace comes from a true worship of God. The dominant word in the last half of Psalm 122 is "peace."

   a. **What do you think Jesus meant when He said, "Peace I leave with you; my peace I give you. I do not give to you as the world gives. Do not let your hearts be troubled and do not be afraid" (John 14:27)?**

      (Jesus gives us a peace that is beyond the peace the world can offer.)

   b. **Let's take a peace inventory. Next to each area of your life, put an X under the word that best describes how often you feel peace.**

	Total Peace	Some Peace	No Peace at all
Relationship with God			
Family life			
Friendships			
School			
Your future			
How you feel about yourself			

   c. **How does the worship of God affect how you feel about your problems and challenges?**

SO WHAT?

The next time you worship:
- Give God your attitude.
- Give God your praise.

Expect great things when you meet with God.
Reflect on His goodness and give Him the praise He deserves and loves to hear.

- Give God your prayers.

Pray for the peace of others and yourself.

The result: You'll find a deeper understanding of worship and enjoy one of the greatest experiences given to us from God.

THINGS TO THINK ABOUT (OPTIONAL)

- Use the questions on page 115 after or as a part of "In the Word."

1. **What makes most worship experiences boring or meaningless?**

2. **What activities do you like best in a worship service? In your personal worship time?**

3. **Why do you think peace could be a direct result of worship?**

PARENT PAGE

- Distribute page to parents.

IN THE WORD

THE PURSUIT OF WORSHIP

Worship—the honor and reverence paid to God

1. Give God your attitude.

   a. Read Psalm 122. What is the attitude of the person speaking in verse 1?

   b. A great philosopher once said, "When it comes to worship we should never ask 'How was it?' We should ask 'How did I do?'" How is this statement different from what most people think of when it comes to worship?

   c. To participate and enjoy a good worship experience we must develop a proper attitude toward worship. How do you prepare for your worship experience?

   d. What specific things can you do to understand and enjoy your worship experience?

Your attitude makes such a difference. Start your next worship experience with a new attitude.

2. Give God your praise.

   a. According to Psalm 122:3,4, why did the tribes of the Lord come to Jerusalem?

   b. Read Psalm 100. How did you feel after you read the verses?

c. What relationship do you find between worship and praise?

....

....

....

d. Why should God receive our praise?

....

....

....

3. Give God your prayers.
   a. Looking again at Psalm 122, what did the writer of this psalm pray for according to verses 6-8?

....

....

....

   b. How is time spent with God in prayer a form of worship?

....

....

....

   c. Reread verses 6-8. The setting is at least 2,500 years ago in Israel. How could you modernize these prayers and
       make them pertinent to your life today?

....

....

....

4. The Product of Worship
   Peace comes from a true worship of God. The dominant word in the last half of Psalm 122 is "peace."
   a. What do you think Jesus meant when He said, "Peace I leave with you; my peace I give you. I do not give to you
       as the world gives. Do not let your hearts be troubled and do not be afraid" (John 14:27)?

....

....

....

b. Let's take a peace inventory. Next to each area of your life, put an *X* under the word that best describes how often you feel peace.

	Total Peace	Some Peace	No Peace at all
Relationship with God			
Family life			
Friendships			
School			
Your future			
How you feel about yourself			

c. How does the worship of God affect how you feel about your problems and challenges?

....

....

....

 O WHAT?

The next time you worship:

- Give God your attitude.   Expect great things when you meet with God.
- Give God your praise.   Reflect on His goodness and give Him the praise He deserves and loves to hear.
- Give God your prayers.   Pray for the peace of others and yourself.

The result: You'll find a deeper understanding of worship and enjoy one of the greatest experiences given to us from God.

THINGS TO THINK ABOUT

1. What makes most worship experiences boring or meaningless?

....

....

....

2. What activities do you like best in a worship service? In your personal worship time?

....

....

....

3. Why do you think peace could be a direct result of worship?

....

....

....

....

PARENT PAGE

A CHECKLIST FOR WORSHIP

There are two types of worship: corporate and personal. Corporate means with other believers and personal, of course, is your own time with God. Both aspects of worship are essential to a good relationship with God.

Check the box below the phrase that best describes your level of participation in each of the four elements of personal worship. Make goals to improve those areas that need work.

Personal Worship

	Improvement Urgent	Improvement Desirable	Acceptable	Excellent
Praise				
Bible study				
Prayer				
Music				

What steps do you need to take to improve your personal worship?

....

....

Check the box below the phrase that best describes your level of participation in each of the six elements of corporate worship. Make goals to improve those areas that need work.

Corporate Worship

	Improvement Urgent	Improvement Desirable	Acceptable	Excellent
Praise				
Sermon				
Prayer				
Music				
Giving				
The Sacraments				

What steps do you need to take to improve your corporate worship?

....

....

Session 6 "Worship" Date ....

117

THE BIBLE

KEY VERSE

"**D**o not let this Book of the Law depart from your mouth; meditate on it day and night, so that you may be careful to do everything written in it. Then you will be prosperous and successful." Joshua 1:8

BIBLICAL BASIS

Joshua 1:8;
Psalm 1; 119:11,105;
Isaiah 26:3; 40:31;
Jeremiah 33:3;
Matthew 6:33;
John 8:31-36; 14:14; 15:11;
   16:33; 17:17;
Philippians 4:6,7,19;
2 Timothy 3:16,17;
1 John 5:14,15

THE BIG IDEA

The Bible plays an important role in our relationships with God. Studying God's Word is essential for spiritual growth.

AIMS OF THIS SESSION

During this session you will guide students to:

• Examine the important role the Bible has in a believer's life;

• Develop a better understanding of the Bible's promises to the believer;

• Implement a regular Scripture-reading time with a better understanding of the Bible's role in their lives.

WARM UP

Following Directions—
An activity to learn more about the students.

TEAM EFFORT— JUNIOR HIGH/ MIDDLE SCHOOL

The What if Game—
A look at the results of not knowing or following biblical principles.

TEAM EFFORT— HIGH SCHOOL

Bible Facts—
A contest of Bible knowledge.

IN THE WORD

The Benefits of Bible Study—
A Bible study on the benefits of studying God's Word.

THINGS TO THINK ABOUT (OPTIONAL)

Questions to get students thinking and talking about their Bible-reading habits.

PARENT PAGE

A tool to get the session into the home and allow parents and young people to discuss the promises found in Scripture.

LEADER'S DEVOTIONAL

Casually paging through a food magazine, witness the adjectives used by those who write. They express a kind of boundless enthusiasm as they describe their food experiences: "Blissful...great...pleasing...perfect...best...particularly good...favorite...fine...ample...superb...." the list could go on and on. Enthusiastic adjectives abound! There is no doubt as one reads the words of those who have tasted that what they are describing is wonderful! It sounds like the best stuff on earth!

But wait. Let's look at that short list of adjectives again. Which of them describes what you tasted today as you sat down to your portion of God's Amazing Meal? Was it a *blissful* time, full of *great* truth and *pleasing* understanding? (Even a non-pleasing new understanding can be good for us!) We already know that God's method for filling our souls and growing our spirits in Him is the *best* food source available. It's *particularly good* when we are famished for something more than the world can offer us, when we are hungry and thirsty for some reality in the midst of a world run amuck, a world where whole publications are given over to delighting the palate and worshiping the stomach!

We could play with the adjectives some more, but you get the point. What did God feed you today? Are you appreciating it, blissfully chewing it slowly so as to reap the full benefit of what He has for you? Are you digesting it, making it part of you in every way, asking the Holy Spirit to show you how to apply God's truth in the smallest details of your life? His Word is the finest, most nourishing food available. And you can have all you want! There are no calories—but the energy available through it is staggering! Don't skip this meal in favor of any of the world's junk-food substitutes. When it comes to your spiritual life, take the best that God wants to give you and eat, eat! (Mary Gross, editor, Gospel Light.)

"To receive any deep, inward profit from the Scripture you must read as I have described. Plunge into the very depths of the words you read until revelation, like a sweet aroma, breaks out upon you."—

Jeanne Guyon,
Experiencing the Depths of Jesus Christ
(Christian Books, 1975)

THE BIBLE

KEY VERSE

"Do not let this Book of the Law depart from your mouth; meditate on it day and night, so that you may be careful to do everything written in it. Then you will be prosperous and successful."
Joshua 1:8

BIBLICAL BASIS

Joshua 1:8; Psalm 1; 119:11,105; Isaiah 26:3; 40:31; Jeremiah 33:3; Matthew 6:33; John 8:31-36; 14:14; 15:11; 16:33; 17:17; Philippians 4:6,7,19; 2 Timothy 3:16,17; 1 John 5:14,15

THE BIG IDEA

The Bible plays an important role in our relationship with God. Studying God's Word is essential for spiritual growth.

WARM UP (5-10 MINUTES)

FOLLOWING DIRECTIONS

- Read aloud the following statements. If students answer yes, have them stand on the right side of the room. If students answer no, have them stand on the left side of the room. If students answer maybe, have them stand in the middle of the room.
- Students share their responses.
  I am someone who would follow the directions when:
  Putting together a new bike.
  My parents tell me to clean the house.
  A teacher gives me a special homework assignment.
  The Bible tells me what to do with my life.
  (As a licensed driver) I'm driving on the highway and no one is looking.

TEAM EFFORT—JUNIOR HIGH/ MIDDLE SCHOOL (15-20 MINUTES)

THE WHAT IF GAME

- Give each student a copy of "The What if Game" on page 123 and a pen or pencil, or display a copy using an overhead projector.
- As a whole group, complete the page.

A Month of Praise and Wisdom

By reading less than 10 minutes a day for one month, you can go through the books of Psalms and Proverbs. The psalms are the beautiful songs of the Hebrew people and the proverbs contain great, practical advice on many aspects of life. All you need to do is read five psalms and one proverb each day and after a month you will have completed two of the greatest books in the Bible. Then you will be ready for a new plan, and you will already have started the positive habit of reading the Bible each day.

The 90-Day Experience

Try an experiment that will change your life! You can read the entire New Testament in less than three months if you'll take 15 minutes a day and read approximately three chapters a day for 90 days. Listed is a format you can use to try this experiment. You'll be excited to see the positive results of incorporating biblical principles into your life.

1.	Matthew 1-4	31.	Acts 4-6
2.	Matthew 5-7	32.	Acts 7-9
3.	Matthew 8-10	33.	Acts 10-12
4.	Matthew 11-13	34.	Acts 13-15
5.	Matthew 14-16	35.	Acts 16-18
6.	Matthew 17-19	36.	Acts 19-21:36
7.	Matthew 20-22	37.	Acts 21:37-25:22
8.	Matthew 23-25	38.	Acts 25:23-28:30
9.	Matthew 26-28	39.	Romans 1-3
10.	Mark 1-3	40.	Romans 4-6
11.	Mark 4-6	41.	Romans 7-8
12.	Mark 7-9	42.	Romans 9-11
13.	Mark 10-12	43.	Romans 12-13
14.	Mark 13-16	44.	Romans 14-16
15.	Luke 1-3	45.	1 Corinthians 1-4
16.	Luke 4-6	46.	1 Corinthians 5-7
17.	Luke 7-9	47.	1 Corinthians 8-11
18.	Luke 10-12	48.	1 Corinthians 12-14
19.	Luke 13-15	49.	1 Corinthians 15-16
20.	Luke 16-18	50.	2 Corinthians 1-3
21.	Luke 19-21	51.	2 Corinthians 4-6
22.	Luke 22-24	52.	2 Corinthians 7-9
23.	John 1-3	53.	2 Corinthians 10-13
24.	John 4-6	54.	Galatians 1-2
25.	John 7-9	55.	Galatians 3-4
26.	John 10-12	56.	Galatians 5-6
27.	John 13-16:4	57.	Ephesians 1-3
28.	John 16:5-18	58.	Ephesians 4-6
29.	John 19-21	59.	Philippians 1-2
30.	Acts 1-3	60.	Philippians 3-4
		61.	Colossians 1-2
		62.	Colossians 3-4
		63.	1 Thessalonians 1-3
		64.	1 Thessalonians 4-5
		65.	2 Thessalonians 1-3
		66.	1 Timothy 1-3
		67.	1 Timothy 4-6
		68.	2 Timothy 1-4
		69.	Titus 1-3
		70.	Philemon
		71.	Hebrews 1-2
		72.	Hebrews 3-4:13
		73.	Hebrews 4:14-7
		74.	Hebrews 8-10
		75.	Hebrews 11-13
		76.	James 1-3:12
		77.	James 3:13-5
		78.	1 Peter 1-3:7
		79.	1 Peter 3:8-5
		80.	2 Peter 1-3
		81.	1 John 1-3:10
		82.	1 John 3:11-5
		83.	2 John; 3 John; Jude
		84.	Revelation 1-3
		85.	Revelation 4-6
		86.	Revelation 7-9
		87.	Revelation 10-12
		88.	Revelation 13-15
		89.	Revelation 16-18
		90.	Revelation 19-22

Devotional Books

In less than 10 minutes a day you can read a devotional book. Usually a devotional book has a Scripture, story, challenge or action steps. Devotional books are written to plant the Word of God in your life and give you practical insight in your walk with God. Your leader has a list of several quality devotional books you can purchase at a Christian bookstore.

THINGS TO THINK ABOUT (OPTIONAL)

- Use the questions on page 137 after or as a part of "In the Word."
1. What are the advantages of reading the Bible daily?

....

2. Why do you think God has given us the Bible to read?

....

3. What keeps you from spending more time in God's Word?

....

PARENT PAGE

- Distribute page to parents.

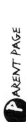

List some of the possible results of not knowing or living out the following biblical principles.

1. **"Love your neighbor as yourself"** (Galatians 5:14).
   a. (Example) Treating other people inconsiderately
   b. ....
   c. ....

2. **"Honor your father and your mother"** (Exodus 20:12).
   a. ....
   b. ....
   c. ....

3. **"Avoid sexual immorality"** (1 Thessalonians 4:3).
   a. ....
   b. ....
   c. ....

TEAM EFFORT—HIGH SCHOOL (15-20 MINUTES)

BIBLE FACTS

- Divide students into groups of three or four.
- Give each group a copy of "Bible Facts" on page 125 and a pen or pencil.
- Students answer questions.
- Each group receives 50 points for the correct answer with the last question being worth 150 points.

1. **How many books in the Bible?**
   (Sixty-six.)
2. **How many books in the Old Testament and how many in the New Testament?**
   (The Old Testament has 39 and the New Testament has 27.)
3. **What language was the New Testament predominantly written in?**
   (Greek.)
4. **What language was the Old Testament predominantly written in?**
   (Hebrew.)
5. **The New Testament is divided into four parts. Name the four parts.**
   (Gospel, acts, letters and revelation.)
6. **The Old Testament is divided into four parts. Name the four parts.**
   (Pentateuch, historical, prophets, wisdom literature.)
7. **Although most of the Old Testament was written in Hebrew and the New Testament in Greek, the common language that Jesus most often spoke was _____.**
   (Aramaic.)

IN THE WORD (25-30 MINUTES)

THE BENEFITS OF BIBLE STUDY

- Divide students into groups of three or four.
- Give each student a copy of "The Benefits of Bible Study" on pages 127 and 129 and a pen or pencil.

— — — — — — Fold — — — — — —

- Students complete the Bible study.
- List of devotional books
  Alive: Daily Devotions for Young People by S. Rickly Christian
  Beefin' Up by Mark Littleton
  Creative Times with God: Building an Adventurous Faith by Doug Fields
  Getting in Touch with God by Jim Burns
  If God Loves Me, Why Can't I Get My Locker Open? by Lorraine Peterson
  If Life Is a Piece of Cake Why Am I Still Hungry? by Doug Fields
  Live It! by Becky Tirabassi
  90 Days Through the New Testament by Jim Burns
  Spirit Wings by Jim Burns

Benefits

According to Joshua 1:8 and Psalm 1, what are the benefits of meditating on (thinking about) God's Word?

(You will be prosperous and successful by doing what God's Word commands. You will be fruitful and your deeds will prosper.)

These Scriptures are not saying that problems will never come our way. But they do seem to say that those who continually place the Word of God in their hearts will have lives that will be enriched with fulfillment and meaning.

Promises

Sometimes we forget the results of placing the Word of God in our lives. Here are some promises that God makes to those who integrate the Word of God into their lives:

Peace
Joy
Truth
Help to Overcome Sin
Direction in Life

Read each Scripture below. Write the word from the list above that best describes the result of reading God's Word.

Result

Psalm 119:11	(Help to Overcome Sin)
Psalm 119:105	(Direction in Life)
John 8:31-36	(Truth)
John 15:11	(Joy)
John 16:33	(Peace)
John 17:17	(Truth)

Action Steps

For a better understanding of why we should read the Bible take a look at 2 Timothy 3:16,17.

What does it say about Scripture?
(Scripture is God-breathed.)

Why is Scripture useful?
(It teaches, rebukes, corrects and trains us in righteousness.)

Since the Bible is God's authority for your life, no doubt you will want to spend more time reading it.

SO WHAT?

To know the Word and to live by it, you will need to take daily time to read the Bible. To develop a habit of Bible reading, it is best to have a consistent time and place.

When and where will you take time to put God's Word to work in your life? You'll need a method. How will you begin? Here are two suggestions:

TEAM EFFORT

THE WHAT IF GAME

List some of the possible results of not knowing or living out the following biblical principles.

1. "Love your neighbor as yourself" (Galatians 5:14).

   a. (Example) Treating other people inconsiderately

   ....

   b. ....

   ....

   c. ....

   ....

   ....

2. "Honor your father and your mother" (Exodus 20:12).

   a. ....

   ....

   b. ....

   ....

   c. ....

   ....

   ....

3. "Avoid sexual immorality" (1 Thessalonians 4:3).

   a. ....

   ....

   b. ....

   ....

   c. ....

   ....

   ....

TEAM EFFORT

BIBLE FACTS

1. How many books in the Bible?

....

....

....

2. How many books in the Old Testament and how many in the New Testament?

....

....

....

3. What language was the New Testament written in?

....

....

....

4. What language was the Old Testament predominantly written in?

....

....

5. The New Testament is divided into four parts. Name the four parts.

....

....

6. The Old Testament is divided into four parts. Name the four parts.

....

....

....

7. Although most of the Old Testament was written in Hebrew and the New Testament in Greek, the common language that Jesus most often spoke was ....

 **IN THE WORD**

THE BENEFITS OF BIBLE STUDY

Benefits

According to Joshua 1:8 and Psalm 1 what are the benefits of meditating on (thinking about) God's Word?

....

These Scriptures are not saying that problems will never come our way. But they do seem to say that those who continually place the Word of God in their hearts will have lives that will be enriched with fulfillment and meaning.

Promises

Sometimes we forget the results of placing the Word of God in our lives. Here are some promises that God makes to those who integrate the Word of God into their lives:

Peace

Joy

Truth

Help to Overcome Sin

Direction in Life

Read each Scripture below. Write the word from the list above that best describes the result of reading God's Word.

Result

Psalm 119:11 ....

Psalm 119:105 ....

John 8:31-36 ....

John 15:11 ....

John 16:33 ....

John 17:17 ....

Action Steps

For a better understanding of why we should read the Bible take a look at 2 Timothy 3:16,17. What does it say about Scripture? ....

....

Why is Scripture useful? ....

....

Since the Bible is God's authority for your life, no doubt you will want to spend more time reading it.

So what?

To know the Word and to live by it, you will need to take daily time to read the Bible. To develop a habit of Bible reading, it is best to have a consistent time and place.

When and where will you take time to put God's Word to work in your life? You'll need a method. How will you begin? Here are two suggestions:

A Month of Praise and Wisdom

By reading less than 10 minutes a day for one month, you can go through the books of Psalms and Proverbs. The psalms are the beautiful songs of the Hebrew people and the proverbs contain great, practical advice on many aspects of life. All you need to do is read five psalms and one proverb each day and after a month you will have completed two of the greatest books in the Bible. Then you will be ready for a new plan and you will already have started the positive habit of reading the Bible each day.

The 90-Day Experience[1]

Try an experiment that will change your life! You can read the entire New Testament in less than three months if you'll take 15 minutes a day and read approximately three chapters a day for 90 days. Listed is a format you can use to try this experiment. You'll be excited to see the positive results of incorporating biblical principles into your life.

1. Matthew 1—4
2. Matthew 5—7
3. Matthew 8—10
4. Matthew 11—13
5. Matthew 14—16
6. Matthew 17—19
7. Matthew 20—22
8. Matthew 23—25
9. Matthew 26—28
10. Mark 1—3
11. Mark 4—6
12. Mark 7—9
13. Mark 10—12
14. Mark 13—16
15. Luke 1—3
16. Luke 4—6
17. Luke 7—9
18. Luke 10—12
19. Luke 13—15
20. Luke 16—18
21. Luke 19—21
22. Luke 22—24
23. John 1—3
24. John 4—6
25. John 7—9
26. John 10—12
27. John 13—16:4
28. John 16:5—18
29. John 19—21
30. Acts 1—3

31. Acts 4—6
32. Acts 7—9
33. Acts 10—12
34. Acts 13—15
35. Acts 16—18
36. Acts 19—21:36
37. Acts 21:37—25:22
38. Acts 25:23—28:30
39. Romans 1—3
40. Romans 4—6
41. Romans 7—8
42. Romans 9—11
43. Romans 12—13
44. Romans 14—16
45. 1 Corinthians 1—4
46. 1 Corinthians 5—7
47. 1 Corinthians 8—11
48. 1 Corinthians 12—14
49. 1 Corinthians 15—16
50. 2 Corinthians 1—3
51. 2 Corinthians 4—6
52. 2 Corinthians 7—9
53. 2 Corinthians 1—13
54. Galatians 1—2
55. Galatians 3—4
56. Galatians 5—6
57. Ephesians 1—3
58. Ephesians 4—6
59. Philippians 1—2
60. Philippians 3—4

61. Colossians 1—2
62. Colossians 3—4
63. 1 Thessalonians 1—3
64. 1 Thessalonians 4—5
65. 2 Thessalonians 1—3
66. 1 Timothy 1—3
67. 1 Timothy 4—6
68. 2 Timothy 1—4
69. Titus 1—3
70. Philemon
71. Hebrews 1—2
72. Hebrews 3—4:13
73. Hebrews 4:14—7
74. Hebrews 8—10
75. Hebrews 11—13
76. James 1—3:12
77. James 3:13—5
78. 1 Peter 1—3:7
79. 1 Peter 3:8—5
80. 2 Peter 1—3
81. 1 John 1—3:10
82. 1 John 3:11—5
83. 2 John; 3 John; Jude
84. Revelation 1—3
85. Revelations 4—6
86. Revelations 7—9
87. Revelation 10—12
88. Revelations 13—15
89. Revelation 16—18
90. Revelation 19—22

Devotional Books

In less than 10 minutes a day you can read a devotional book. Usually a devotional book has a Scripture, story, challenge or action steps. Devotional books are written to plant the Word of God in your life and give you practical insight in your walk with God. Your leader has a list of several quality devotional books you can purchase at a Christian bookstore.

Note

1. Jim Burns, *90 Days Through the New Testament* (Ventura, CA: Regal Books, 1990), pp. 15-135. Used by permission.

THINGS TO THINK ABOUT

1. What are the advantages of reading the Bible daily?

....

....

....

2. Why do you think God has given us the Bible to read?

....

....

....

3. What keeps you from spending more time in God's Word?

....

....

....

 PARENT PAGE

The Promises of God

Some people have estimated that there are over 3,000 promises in the Bible. Many of those promises are related to the area of prayer. Listed below are a number of promises. Read the Scripture. Then write out the promise and how it affects your life.

The Scripture	The Promise	How It Affects My Life
Isaiah 26:3		
Isaiah 40:31		
Jeremiah 33:3		
Matthew 6:33		
John 14:14		
Philippians 4:6,7		
Philippians 4:19		
1 John 5:14,15		

Session 7 "The Bible" Date ....

GETTING YOUR SPIRITUAL LIFE IN SHAPE

Key Verses

"Do you not know that in a race all the runners run, but only one gets the prize? Run in such a way as to get the prize. Everyone who competes in the games goes into strict training. They do it to get a crown that will not last; but we do it to get a crown that will last forever. Therefore I do not run like a man running aimlessly; I do not fight like a man beating the air. No, I beat my body and make it my slave so that after I have preached to others, I myself will not be disqualified for the prize."
1 Corinthians 9:24-27

Biblical Basis

1 Corinthians 9:24-27;
Colossians 3:13;
Ephesians 6:10-18;
1 Timothy 4:7

The Big Idea

Although our salvation is a free gift, there are scriptural principles that lead to spiritual growth and to getting our spiritual lives in shape.

Aims of This Session

During this session you will guide students to:
• Examine the important elements of spiritual growth in the believer;
• Discover how to win the battle between the spirit and the flesh;
• Implement a plan to get their spiritual lives in shape by using specific goals.

Warm Up

Sit Down If—
An activity to get to know students.

Team Effort—Junior High/Middle School

Goals—
Students develop some short- and long-term goals.

Team Effort—High School

Gearing Up for the Battle—
A look at the armor of God.

In the Word

Your Mind Matters—
A Bible study on developing and achieving spiritual goals.

Things to Think About (OPTIONAL)

Questions to get students thinking and talking about getting their spiritual lives in shape.

Parent Page

A tool to get the session into the home and allow parents and young people to evaluate their spiritual lives.

LEADER'S DEVOTIONAL

We've all done it. When we notice that our clothes no longer fit or the bathroom scale is about to reach maximum capacity, we decide that we will *do* something! We buy exercise machines or new jogging shoes, sure that that will motivate us, commit us to our goal—increased physical fitness. But most of us would have to admit that sometime, somehow our goals shift and we find ourselves spending less and less time in "exercise mode"!

With that in mind, we can see why Paul told the Corinthians, "Run in such a way as to get the prize." It's very easy to let our daily Divine Training Program slide a little bit. After all, being in church so much counts as some substitute for time spent alone with God, doesn't it? (We all know the answer!) We all know the vital importance of time spent with God, talking to Him, listening to Him, reading His Word. We must learn to become good soldiers of Jesus Christ, living lives of victory. And a hit-or-miss approach to our relationships with God will not yield such a powerful result. Just as with the painful realities of physical training, we have to commit to a goal. A new program or method may not create that commitment. (Like the new exercise machine, it may lie unused in a corner, too.)

So, how can we possibly run, train, exercise ourselves spiritually in such a way as to get the prize? If we so often fail at physical training programs, we know the spirit is willing but the flesh is weak! What can we do? Did God set us up, doomed always to clutch after a life of victory, feeling guilty over our failures or spiritually superior over our successes?

God didn't set us up. It's just that in our decisions to *do something*, we sometimes forget this vital truth: Having begun our lives in Jesus by the power of His Spirit, we must remember that the only way to keep up the pace, to stay in shape, is by that *same* Power! In John 15:5 (*NKJV*), Jesus told His closest friends, "Without Me, you can do nothing." Consistent, powerful time spent with God can *only* come through *His* power, not ours! And He is always waiting and able to help us! When we want to stay in bed or skip devotions today, He's waiting. We need to remember to stop and say, "Lord, without You I can't do this. Please make me able to get up, to pray, to spend time with You. I know I am dependent on You, Lord. Please do whatever You need to do in me so I am able! " Top-notch spiritual condition, ready for whatever God wants us to do, is an attainable goal—if we will commit to asking Him to make us able. (Mary Gross, editor, Gospel Light.)

"In short, [nondiscipleship] costs exactly that abundance of life Jesus said he came to bring.—

Dallas Willard, *The Spirit of Disciplines* (Harper & Row, 1989).

BIBLE TUCK-IN™

Getting Your Spiritual Life in Shape

Key Verses

"Do you not know that in a race all the runners run, but only one gets the prize? Run in such a way as to get the prize. Everyone who competes in the games goes into strict training. They do it to get a crown that will not last; but we do it to get a crown that will last forever. Therefore I do not run like a man running aimlessly; I do not fight like a man beating the air. No, I beat my body and make it my slave so that after I have preached to others, I myself will not be disqualified for the prize." 1 Corinthians 9:24-27

Biblical Basis

1 Corinthians 9:24-27; Colossians 3:13; Ephesians 6:10-18; 1 Timothy 4:7

The Big Idea

Although our salvation is a free gift, there are scriptural principles that lead to spiritual growth and to getting our spiritual lives in shape.

Warm Up (5-10 Minutes)

Sit Down If

- Have students stand up.
- Read the following instructions:
  Sit down if...
    1. you didn't use deodorant today.
    2. you sing in the shower.
    3. you are really good looking.
    4. *stand up* if the person next to you just sat down and was wrong.
    5. your nose is running and you don't have a handkerchief.
    6. you are a girl and you didn't shave your legs this month.
    7. you are a guy and you did shave your legs this month.
    8. you like anchovies on your pizza.
    9. you would like to develop athletic ability.

---

d. What common elements are there in the discipline of an athlete and spiritual discipline?
(Each has a goal in mind and works daily toward that goal.)

e. What will it take for you to become a more spiritually disciplined person?

3. We need to know our goal.
What was Paul's goal in 1 Corinthians 9:24-27?
(To win the race.)

So What?

Write one thing that you can do this week to get your spiritual life in shape.

Remember we're all running the race—in the process. It's a marathon, so just keep at it!

Things to Think About (optional)

- Use the questions on page 147 after or as a part of "In the Word."

1. What keeps people from developing spiritual discipline in their lives?

2. What does this phrase mean: "He or she who aims at nothing gets there every time"?

3. Who do you know who has his or her spiritual life in shape? What steps did he or she take to get in shape?

4. What characteristics do you see in his or her life?

Parent Page

- Distribute page to parents.

GOALS

• Divide students into groups of three or four.
• Give each student a copy of "Goals" on page 139 and a pen or pencil.
• Students share their goals.

Goals are important. If you don't have goals how will you ever know if you've accomplished what you want to be and do in life?
Check the answer that best describes you.
My goals in life are:

_____ unclear.
_____ seldom obtained.
_____ a real priority.
_____ what goals?
_____ clear.
_____ achieved regularly.

Here is an important exercise in goal setting. Write out a short-term (in one year) goal and a long-term (in five to seven years) goal for each area of your life listed below. Then, most importantly, act upon those goals.

Spiritual Goals
Short-term
....
Long-term
....

Relationship Goals (family and friends)
Short-term
....
Long-term
....

School or Career Goals
Short-term
....
Long-term
....

Share your goals in your group.
Which goal in each section can you begin working on today?

TEAM EFFORT—HIGH SCHOOL (15-20 MINUTES)

GEARING UP FOR THE BATTLE

• Give each student a copy of "Gearing Up for the Battle" on page 141 and a pen or pencil.
• Students complete the drawing individually.
• Divide students into groups of three or four.
• Students answer the question.

Read Ephesians 6:10-18. Draw the armor of God on the person below.
How is each piece of armor used in a spiritual battle?

---

1. Belt of truth
(Relates every thought to God's truth.)
2. Breastplate of righteousness
(Protects against Satan's accusations of your worth before God.)
3. Shoes of the gospel of peace
(Protects against the devil's divisiveness when you try to bring peace.)
4. Shield of faith
(Believing God and His Word against the devil's lies.)
5. Helmet of salvation
(Protects your mind and assures you of the ultimate victory, salvation.)
6. Sword of the Spirit
(Speaking God's truth against Satan's lies.)

IN THE WORD (25-30 MINUTES)

DISCIPLINING YOUR SPIRITUAL LIFE

• Divide students into groups of three or four.
• Give each student a copy of "Disciplining Your Spiritual Life" on pages 143 and 145 and a pen or pencil, or display a copy using an overhead projector.
• Students complete the Bible study.

Do you not know that in a race all the runners run, but only one gets the prize? Run in such a way as to get the prize. Everyone who competes in the games goes into strict training. They do it to get a crown that will not last; but we do it to get a crown that will last forever. Therefore I do not run like a man running aimlessly; I do not fight like a man beating the air. No, I beat my body and make it my slave so that after I have preached to others, I myself will not be disqualified for the prize (1 Corinthians 9:24-27).

In a way, 1 Corinthians 9:24-27 is the apostle Paul's philosophy of life. Can you imagine him saying, "There is the easy road to life that gets you nowhere and there is the disciplined road that leads to spiritual victory."
Many Christians let their spiritual lives get out of shape. They get lazy and don't exercise their spiritual muscles and their relationships with God become shallow.
If you desire to get your spiritual life in shape, take a closer look at Paul's philosophy of life found in 1 Corinthians 9:24-27.

Paul's Philosophy of Life
1. Life is a battle.
a. Read 1 Corinthians 9:24-27. What type of battle is Paul describing?
(A personal, spiritual battle.)
b. What battles are you facing?
c. What would it take to win the battle? (First Corinthians 9 uses the phrase "to win the race.")

2. To win the battle demands discipline.
a. How does 1 Corinthians 9:25 relate to this point?
(To win requires strict training.)
b. What is the principle Paul shared with Timothy in 1 Timothy 4:7?
(Train yourself to be godly.)
c. Complete this sentence by circling the answer that best fits your life. I consider myself a disciplined person:
1. most of the time.
2. some of the time.
3. seldom.

TEAM EFFORT

GOALS

Goals are important. If you don't have goals how will you ever know if you've accomplished what you want to be and do in life?

Check the answer that describes you best.

My goals in life are:

.... unclear.

.... seldom obtained.

.... a real priority.

.... what goals?

.... clear.

.... achieved regularly.

Here is an important exercise in goal setting. Write out a short-term (in one year) goal and a long-term (in five to seven years) goal for each area of your life listed below. Then, most importantly, act upon those goals.

Spiritual Goals

Short-term ....

....

Long-term ....

....

Relationship Goals (family and friends)

Short-term ....

....

Long-term ....

....

School or Career Goals

Short-term ....

....

Long-term ....

....

Share your goals in your group.

Which goal in each section can you begin working on today? ....

....

....

TEAM EFFORT

GEARING UP FOR THE BATTLE

Read Ephesians 6:10-18. Draw the armor of God on the person below.
How is each piece of armor used in a spiritual battle?

1. Belt of truth

....

....

....

2. Breastplate of righteousness

....

....

....

3. Shoes of the gospel of peace

....

....

....

4. Shield of faith

....

....

....

5. Helmet of salvation

....

....

....

6. Sword of the Spirit

....

....

....

IN THE WORD

DISCIPLINING YOUR SPIRITUAL LIFE

Do you not know that in a race all the runners run, but only one gets the prize? Run in such a way as to get the prize. Everyone who competes in the games goes into strict training. They do it to get a crown that will not last; but we do it to get a crown that will last forever. Therefore I do not run like a man running aimlessly; I do not fight like a man beating the air. No, I beat my body and make it my slave so that after I have preached to others, I myself will not be disqualified for the prize (1 Corinthians 9:24-27).

In a way, 1 Corinthians 9:24-27 is the apostle Paul's philosophy of life. Can you imagine him saying, "There is the easy road to life that gets you nowhere and there is the disciplined road that leads to spiritual victory."

Many Christians let their spiritual lives get out of shape. They get lazy and don't exercise their spiritual muscles and their relationships with God become shallow.

If you desire to get your spiritual life in shape, take a closer look at Paul's philosophy of life found in 1 Corinthians 9:24-27.

Paul's Philosophy of Life

1. Life is a battle.

    a. Read 1 Corinthians 9:24-27. What type of battle is Paul describing? ....

    ....

    ....

    b. What battles are you facing? ....

    ....

    ....

    c. What would it take to win the battle? (First Corinthians 9 uses the phrase "to win the race.")

    ....

    ....

2. To win the battle demands discipline.

    a. How does 1 Corinthians 9:25 relate to this point? ....

    ....

    b. What is the principle Paul shared with Timothy in 1 Timothy 4:7? ....

    ....

    ....

c. Complete this sentence by circling the answer that best fits your life. I consider myself a disciplined person:
    1. most of the time.
    2. some of the time.
    3. seldom.

d. What common elements are there in the discipline of an athlete and spiritual discipline? ....
    ....
    ....
    ....

e. What will it take for you to become a more spiritually disciplined person?
    ....
    ....

3. We need to know our goal.

    What was Paul's goal in 1 Corinthians 9:24-27? ....
    ....
    ....

So WHAT?

Write one thing that you can do this week to get your spiritual life in shape.

....

Remember we're all running the race—in the process. It's a marathon, so just keep at it!

*T*HINGS TO THINK ABOUT

1. What keeps people from developing spiritual discipline in their lives?

....

....

....

2. What does this phrase mean: "He or she who aims at nothing gets there every time"?

....

....

....

3. Who do you know who has his or her spiritual life in shape? What steps did he or she take to get in shape?

....

....

....

4. What characteristics do you see in his or her life?

....

....

....

PARENT PAGE

And whatever you do, whether in word or deed, do it all in the name of the Lord Jesus, giving thanks to God the Father through him (Colossians 3:17).

How much of your time and attention does God want?

....

....

....

....

Does God have your time and attention in these areas?

	All of it	Most of it	Some of it	None of it
Prayer	☐	☐	☐	☐
Bible reading	☐	☐	☐	☐
Living like a servant	☐	☐	☐	☐
Giving	☐	☐	☐	☐
Friendships	☐	☐	☐	☐
Sharing Christ with others	☐	☐	☐	☐
Loving your family	☐	☐	☐	☐

What can you as a family do to help each other improve in these areas?

....

....

....

....

....

Session 8 "Getting Your Spiritual Life in Shape" Date..........................

ELEMENTS OF PRAYER

LEADER'S PEP TALK

I really like this section! I enjoyed doing these experiences and Bible studies with students. Here's why: I'm convinced most young people (adults, too) only pray the "God give me" prayer. Most people have the elements of prayer all messed up. We spend the vast majority of our time and energy in asking for things and telling God what to do. When most people pray, *they* become the master and God becomes the servant. "God do this. God provide that. God go there." However, true prayer is much more than asking (although asking is important as you see in Session 12).

If you would take a look at my daily journal you'd see that after I've read some Scripture and spent a few moments just listening, I then move into ACTS: Adoration—Confession—Thanksgiving—Supplication. This little formula that I do on a daily basis, and that is taught in these sessions, has revolutionized my relationship with God.

I believe you can teach your students the ACTS prayer method as well. Praise frees our spirit to be in touch with our Creator. Thanksgiving gives us a proper attitude. Confession and forgiveness give us a right relationship with God, and asking our loving heavenly Father for His will reminds us of the depth of God's love for us.

If your students aren't familiar with praise, thanksgiving and confession, then you have the opportunity to teach them key biblical principles. You are placing some of the spiritual secrets of the master teacher Jesus at their feet.

You'll notice I am using a lot of psalms in this section. As you probably know, the psalms were the songs of the Hebrew people. Hopefully this section will provide a foundation for stronger and deeper elements of prayer than some of your students have ever experienced.

Don't get discouraged if some of your students aren't ready for a deeper communication with God. You are still placing before them spiritual truths that "will not return void" (see Isaiah 55:11). Let me leave you with this great thought from Richard Foster,

> Healthy prayer necessitates frequent experiences of the
> common, earthy, run-of-the-mill variety. Like walks, and

talks, and good wholesome laughter. Like work in the yard, and chitchat with the neighbors, and washing windows. Like loving our spouse, and playing with our kids, and working with our colleagues. To be spiritually fit to scale the Himalayas of the spirit, we need regular exercise in the hills and valleys of ordinary life.[1]

Note

1. Richard J. Foster, *Prayer: Finding the Heart's True Home*
   (San Francisco, CA: Harper Collins, 1992), p. XII.

PRAISE

KEY VERSE

"**L**et everything that has breath praise the LORD." Psalm 150:6

BIBLICAL BASIS

Psalm 34:1-10; 144—150

THE BIG IDEA

Praise is the purest form of worship. Praise frees up our spirits to really live for God.

AIMS OF THIS SESSION

During this session you will guide students to:

- Examine how praise is an important element in corporate and private prayer times;
- Discover how to use the principles of praise in their lives and relationships with God;
- Implement praise into their every day lives this week.

WARM UP

Everyday Praise—
Young people share the praise in their lives.

TEAM EFFORT— JUNIOR HIGH/ MIDDLE SCHOOL

Recognizing Praise—
An evaluation of praise in their church and youth group.

TEAM EFFORT— HIGH SCHOOL

Why Not Praise Him?—
Students brainstorm reasons for praising God.

IN THE WORD

A Psalm of Praise—
A Bible study on God's instruction on praise.

THINGS TO THINK ABOUT (OPTIONAL)

Questions to get students thinking and talking about praising God.

PARENT PAGE

A tool to get the session into the home and allow parents and young people to discuss themes of praise. God gives to prayers.

LEADER'S DEVOTIONAL

Among the elements of prayer, praise and adoration sound extremely spiritual. And they are! But praise is also the place in our prayer lives where we can grab hold of the spiritual and the actual at the same time and see them in a vivid way. When we praise God, we have to stop and look at what God has already done. Here before us are actual, visible answers from God, whether things He has sent or situations He has changed—provided by thoroughly spiritual means! That gives us reason to remember that He is good, far better to us than we would ever be to ourselves.

When we stop to consider God's goodness and the astonishing answers He has made to our prayers, what effect does it have on us? First, we are humbled and grateful at the amazing grace He shows us every day. We know we don't deserve even a tiny portion of this love. This only opens our hearts to thankfulness. But we are also then emboldened to go back into the throne room of God with gusto! We're excited, ready to climb up on His knee and talk to Him some more because we know He listens! And that is precisely what He wants.

Praise is also a moment-by-moment kind of prayer in itself. When we begin to praise God, every time we receive a gem from His hand—a small but delightful token of His enormous affection for us—we are opening yet another dimension in our daily walk with Him. He wants us to notice what He is doing and praise Him for it, not because He's in need of hearing our praise but because He knows that it takes us to new levels of awareness of *Him* even in the midst of our daily business. Whether you praise God in song, in words from your heart or simply in unspoken joy, you are *with* Him in those moments. And that is the essence of relationship with the One who loves you and desires to have you close to His heart! (Mary Gross, editor, Gospel Light.)

"Adoration is 'loving back.' For in the prayer of adoration we love God for himself, for his very being, for his radiant joy."—

Douglas V. Steere,
Prayer and Worship
(Friends United
Press, 1978)

PRAISE

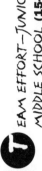

KEY VERSE

"Let everything that has breath praise the LORD." Psalm 150:6

BIBLICAL BASIS

Psalm 34:1-10; 144—150

THE BIG IDEA

Praise is the purest form of worship. Praise frees up our spirits to really live for God.

WARM UP (5-10 MINUTES)

EVERYDAY PRAISE

- Display a copy of "Everyday Praise" on page 157 using an overhead projector.
- Divide students into groups of three or four.
- Students discuss questions.

1. What is praise?

2. How do we use it in our everyday lives? (Example, praising a dog for something well done.)

3. How do we use it with God?

4. Why do you think God deserves our praise?

TEAM EFFORT—JUNIOR HIGH/MIDDLE SCHOOL (15-20 MINUTES)

RECOGNIZING PRAISE

- Divide students into groups of three or four.
- Give each student a copy of "Recognizing Praise" on page 159 and a pen or pencil.
- Students complete page.
- Have two groups join and share responses.

Praise is an important part of our worship celebration. For many people, the weekly worship service has become nothing but a boring ritual. However, when we infuse praise into our worship service we can experience a new level of worship.

---------- Fold ----------

THINGS TO THINK ABOUT (OPTIONAL)

- Use the questions on page 167 after or as a part of "In the Word."

1. Why is it important to have a consistent attitude of praise to God in our hearts?

2. How can praising God positively affect the other areas of your spiritual life (thanksgiving, confession, servanthood, etc.)?

3. If Jesus were physically sitting next to you right now, what do you think He would say to you about how you praise Him?

4. Praise can lift our hearts up to the very throne of God. What are some difficulties that keep you from that special and holy place of God?

PARENT PAGE

- Distribute page to parents.

List below as many acts of praise to God you can find in your worship service at church and in your youth group.

....

....

TEAM EFFORT—HIGH SCHOOL (15-20 MINUTES)

WHY NOT PRAISE HIM?

- Divide students into groups of three or four.
- Give each student a copy of "Why Not Praise Him?" on page 161 and a pen or pencil.
- Students complete page.
- As a whole group, discuss responses. Post responses as a reminder in your room.

Praise is the purest form of worship. When we begin to have an attitude of praise, we free our spirits to live for God. There is nothing more exciting than the experience of lifting up our hearts to God in praise.

Brainstorm as many reasons as you possibly can to offer God your praise. List them on this page.

IN THE WORD (25-30 MINUTES)

A PSALM OF PRAISE

- Divide students into groups of three or four.
- Give each student a copy of "A Psalm of Praise" on pages 163, 165 and 167 and a pen or pencil.
- Students complete the Bible study.

Take this great psalm of praise verse by verse and apply it to your life today by answering the questions below each verse.

Praise the Lord. Praise God in his sanctuary; praise him in his mighty heavens (Psalm 150:1).

1. **Where do we praise God?**

2. **Does our church find times every week to praise Him? How?**

3. **What strength will we find when we learn to praise the Lord?**

(We find that we are are connected to the One who gives us strength.)

Praise him for his acts of power; praise him for his surpassing greatness (Psalm 150:2).

4. **What are acts of power?**

(God acting in power over all other beings and things.)

5. **If God already knows how great He is, why do we need to tell Him?**

(Because He commands us, and He desires us to be blessed through praising Him.)

Praise him with the sounding of the trumpet, praise him with the harp and lyre, praise him with tambourine and dancing, praise him with the strings and flute, praise him with the clash of cymbals, praise him with resounding cymbals (Psalm 150:3–5).

6. **When the psalm was written, these were the instruments to praise God. How does music and song relate to praise?**

(Music and song are expressive, creative and common ways to praise God.)

Let everything that has breath praise the Lord. Praise the Lord (Psalm 150:6).

Fold

---

7. **Why should everything that breathes praise the Lord?**

8. **How can we apply this verse to our daily lives?**

("Everything" needs to recognize God and give Him what He deserves—praise.)

I will extol the Lord at all times; his praise will always be on my lips. My soul will boast in the Lord; let the afflicted hear and rejoice. Glorify the Lord with me; let us exalt his name together. I sought the Lord, and he answered me; he delivered me from all my fears. Those who look to him are radiant; their faces are never covered with shame. This poor man called, and the Lord heard him; he saved him out of all his troubles. The angel of the Lord encamps around those who fear him, and he delivers them. Taste and see that the Lord is good; blessed is the man who takes refuge in him. Fear the Lord, you his saints, for those who fear him lack nothing. The lions may grow weak and hungry, but those who seek the Lord lack no good thing (Psalm 34:1–10).

9. **According to this psalm, how often should we praise the Lord?**

(Always.)

10. **List the spiritual principles you find in Psalm 34:1–10 and Psalm 150.**

....

SO WHAT?

Now take three principles you found in Psalm 34:1–10 and Psalm 150 that you can apply to your life this week. Write alongside the principle how you can use it.

Spiritual Principle One ....

How ....

Spiritual Principle Two ....

How ....

Spiritual Principle Three ....

How ....

WARM UP

EVERYDAY PRAISE

1. What is praise?

....

....

....

2. How do we use it in our everyday lives? (Example, praising a dog for something well done.)

....

....

....

3. How do we use it with God?

....

....

....

4. Why do you think God deserves our praise?

....

....

....

....

 EAM EFFORT

RECOGNIZING PRAISE

Praise is an important part of our worship celebration. For many people, the weekly worship service has become nothing but a boring ritual. However, when we infuse praise into our worship service we can experience a new level of worship.

List below as many acts of praise to God you can find in your worship service at church and in your youth group.

....

....

....

....

....

....

....

....

....

....

....

....

....

....

....

....

....

....

 TEAM EFFORT

WHY NOT PRAISE HIM?

Let everything that breathes praise the LORD (Psalm 150:6).

Praise is the purest form of worship. When we begin to have an attitude of praise, we free our spirits to live for God. There is nothing more exciting than the experience of lifting up our hearts to God in praise.

Brainstorm as many reasons as you possibly can to offer God your praise. List them on this page.

....

....

....

....

....

....

....

....

....

....

....

....

....

....

N THE WORD

A PSALM OF PRAISE

Take this great psalm of praise verse by verse and apply it to your life today by answering the questions below each verse.

> Praise the LORD. Praise God in his sanctuary; praise him in his mighty heavens (Psalm 150:1).

1. Where do we praise God?

....

....

2. Does our church find times every week to praise Him? How?

....

....

3. What strength will we find when we learn to praise the Lord?

....

....

> Praise him for his acts of power; praise him for his surpassing greatness (Psalm 150:2).

4. What are acts of power?

....

....

....

5. If God already knows how great He is why do we need to tell Him?

....

> Praise him with the sounding of the trumpet, praise him with the harp and lyre, praise him with tambourine and dancing, praise him with the strings and flute, praise him with the clash of cymbals, praise him with resounding cymbals (Psalm 150:3-5).

163

6. When the psalm was written, these were the instruments to praise God. How does music and song relate to praise?

....

....

Let everything that has breath praise the Lord. Praise the Lord (Psalm 150:6).

7. Why should everything that breathes praise the Lord?

....

....

8. How can we apply this verse to our daily lives?

....

....

I will extol the LORD at all times; his praise will always be on my lips. My soul will boast in the LORD; let the afflicted hear and rejoice. Glorify the LORD with me; let us exalt his name together. I sought the LORD, and he answered me; he delivered me from all my fears. Those who look to him are radiant; their faces are never covered with shame. This poor man called, and the LORD heard him; he saved him out of all his troubles. The angel of the LORD encamps around those who fear him, and he delivers them.

Taste and see that the LORD is good; blessed is the man who takes refuge in him. Fear the LORD, you his saints, for those who fear him lack nothing. The lions may grow weak and hungry, but those who seek the LORD lack no good thing (Psalm 34:1-10).

9. According to this psalm, how often should we praise the Lord?

....

....

....

10. List the spiritual principles you find in Psalm 34:1-10 and Psalm 150.

....

....

....

SO WHAT?

Now take three principles you found in Psalm 34:1-10 and Psalm 150 that you can apply to your life this week. Write alongside the principle how you can use it.

Spiritual Principle One ....

....

How ....

....

Spiritual Principle Two ....

....

How ....

....

Spiritual Principle Three ....

....

How ....

....

THINGS TO THINK ABOUT

1. Why is it important to have a consistent attitude of praise to God in our hearts?

....

....

2. How can praising God positively affect the other areas of your spiritual life (thanksgiving, confession, servanthood, etc.)?

....

....

3. If Jesus were physically sitting next to you right now, what do you think He would say to you about how you praise Him?

....

....

4. Praise can lift our hearts up to the very throne of God. What are some difficulties that keep you from that special and holy place of God?

....

....

167

PRAISE

The last seven psalms in the Bible are all psalms of praise to God. As a family, read through these psalms and find a theme for each psalm of praise. You can use a direct verse from the psalm or use your own words.

Psalm 144 ....

Psalm 145 ....

Psalm 146 ....

Psalm 147 ....

Psalm 148 ....

Psalm 149 ....

Psalm 150 ....

Have each family member share a reason they are filled with praise to the Lord. Now take a few moments to praise God for the reasons that were shared. You may want to go around in a circle and say, "Lord, I praise You because...."

Session 9 "Praise" Date ....

CONFESSION AND FORGIVENESS

KEY VERSES

"But Jesus went to the Mount of Olives. At dawn he appeared again in the temple courts, where all the people gathered around him, and he sat down to teach them. The teachers of the law and the Pharisees brought in a woman caught in adultery. They made her stand before the group and said to Jesus, 'Teacher, this woman was caught in the act of adultery. In the Law Moses commanded us to stone such women. Now what do you say?' They were using this question as a trap, in order to have a basis for accusing him.

"But Jesus bent down and started to write on the ground with his finger. When they kept on questioning him, he straightened up and said to them, 'If any one of you is without sin, let him be the first to throw a stone at her.' Again he stooped down and wrote on the ground.

"At this, those who heard began to go away one at a time, the older ones first, until only Jesus was left, with the woman still standing there. Jesus straightened up and asked her, 'Woman, where are they? Has no one condemned you?'

"'No one, sir,' she said.

"'Then neither do I condemn you,' Jesus declared. 'Go now and leave your life of sin.'" John 8:1-11

BIBLICAL BASIS

Psalm 86:5;
Isaiah 1:18;
John 8:1-11;
Hebrews 10:17;
1 John 1:9

THE BIG IDEA

The spiritual act of confession is an essential element in our prayer lives. The natural result of confession is forgiveness in Christ.

AIMS OF THIS SESSION

During this session you will guide students to:

• Examine the exciting and important spiritual principles for confession and forgiveness;

• Develop a better understanding of the principles for confession and forgiveness in their lives;

• Implement the needed changes to include confession with an emphasis on forgiveness in their prayer lives.

WARM UP
True Confessions—

An opportunity for young people to share.

TEAM EFFORT— JUNIOR HIGH/ MIDDLE SCHOOL
Confessing Our Sins—

An activity to confess their sins to God.

TEAM EFFORT— HIGH SCHOOL
The Blood of Christ—

A look at the significance of blood in forgiveness.

IN THE WORD
Good News for Those Who Are Imperfect—

A Bible study on God's gift of forgiveness.

THINGS TO THINK ABOUT (OPTIONAL)

Questions to get students thinking and talking about forgiveness and confession.

PARENT PAGE

A tool to get the session into the home and allow parents and young people to discuss family forgiveness.

LEADER'S DEVOTIONAL

We've all heard it: "That makes me sick!" The exclamation is usually accompanied by a "yuk" expression on the face and a tightness in the stomach. What "turns your stomach"? A disturbing neighbor? A radical or a racist? A prostitute? A biker? A drug addict? If we haven't named your particular stomach-turner yet, keep thinking. What makes you say "Yuk!" inside?

The Pharisees brought a woman caught in adultery to Jesus, no doubt making "yuk faces." She really turned *their* stomachs! But Jesus moved to help them get over such sickness, using the principle expressed in James 5:16: "Confess your sins to each other and pray for each other so that you may be healed." Squatting in the middle of this crowd full of tense self-righteousness, He began to write in the dust. Perhaps He wrote names of women with whom the accusers had committed adultery. But whatever He wrote gave all of the woman's accusers a chance to either confess their own sin and identify with this adulteress as fellow sinners—or walk away silent.

On the other hand, the woman was the picture of confession, for the whole world seemed to know about her sin. Utterly humbled and defenseless, she lay at the feet of the Lord Jesus. And what did He say to this one? "I don't condemn you; go your way and sin no more!"

What does it take for us to be truly healed from our pride and self-righteousness? How do we get over our own "turned stomachs" to deal with our sometimes blind refusal to notice our own sin? Confession. Confession to God first and to others also, both to gain forgiveness and to release that healing James describes. The alternative is to walk away silent, letting the sin we hold eat away until it leaves a hole in our spiritual armor where Satan will send his darts to deeply injure us and leave a wound where bitterness festers.

So we confess to God and to each other. What good does such healing do? Why does God want healed people anyway? James goes on to tell us why: because the fervent prayer of a righteous person is powerful and effective. God wants righteous (spiritually healthy) people who can prevail in prayer. The battle that is going on all around us needs people who can pray with power! (Mary Gross, editor, Gospel Light.)

"God does not ask us to confess our sins because He needs to know we have sinned, but because He knows that *we* need to know we have sinned."—

Dick Eastman,
*The Hour That
Changes the World*
(Baker Book
House, 1978)

BIBLE **TUCK-IN**™

CONFESSION AND FORGIVENESS

 **KEY VERSES**

"But Jesus went to the Mount of Olives. At dawn he appeared again in the temple courts, where all the people gathered around him, and he sat down to teach them. The teachers of the law and the Pharisees brought in a woman caught in adultery. They made her stand before the group and said to Jesus, 'Teacher, this woman was caught in the act of adultery. In the Law Moses commanded us to stone such women. Now what do you say?' They were using this question as a trap, in order to have a basis for accusing him.

"But Jesus bent down and started to write on the ground with his finger. When they kept on questioning him, he straightened up and said to them, 'If any one of you is without sin, let him be the first to throw a stone at her.' Again he stooped down and wrote on the ground.

"At this, those who heard began to go away one at a time, the older ones first, until only Jesus was left, with the woman still standing there. Jesus straightened up and asked her, 'Woman, where are they? Has no one condemned you?'

"'No one, sir,' she said.

"'Then neither do I condemn you,' Jesus declared. 'Go now and leave your life of sin.'"

John 8:1-11

 **BIBLICAL BASIS**

Psalm 86:5; Isaiah 1:18; John 8:1-11; Hebrews 10:17; 1 John 1:9

THE BIG IDEA

The spiritual act of confession is an essential element in our prayer lives. The natural result of confession is forgiveness in Christ.

WARM UP (5-10 MINUTES)

TRUE CONFESSIONS
- Display a copy of "True Confessions" on page 175 using an overhead projector.
- Divide students into groups of three or four.
- Each students chooses one of the statements to complete.
My most embarrassing moment was:

Something very few people know about me is:

If I could go anywhere in the world I would go to:

— — — — — — — — — — — — — — Fold — — — — — — — — — — — — — — —

The word "confess" actually means to agree. Confessing your sins to God is agreeing with God that you, like everyone else, fall short of perfection.

Read these verses on confession and forgiveness, and discuss what they mean.

1 John 1:9

Psalm 86:5

Isaiah 1:18

Hebrews 10:17

SO WHAT?

For I will forgive their wickedness and will remember their sins no more (Jeremiah 31:34).

According to this verse what will Christ do with your confessed sins?

What keeps you from taking a few moments right now and confessing your sins to the Lord?

THINGS TO THINK ABOUT (OPTIONAL)
- Use the questions on page 181 after or as a part of "In the Word."
1. Why is it easier to accept God's forgiveness than forgive ourselves?

2. What makes confession to another person such a powerful experience? (See James 5:16.)

3. Where does the idea of repentance come into the picture of forgiveness?

PARENT PAGE
- Distribute page to parents.

If I could do or be anything it would be:

If I could choose to have a gift it would be:

TEAM EFFORT—JUNIOR HIGH/MIDDLE SCHOOL (15-20 MINUTES)

CONFESSING OUR SINS
- As a whole group, complete the following:

Read 1 John 1:8-10.

Define the word "confession."

What does it mean to confess your sins?

What does this verse say about God and prayer?

On a sheet of newsprint, have students write with a felt pen graffiti style as many sins as you can think of. Then, using a red marker, you write "FORGIVEN" across the page.
- Give each student a piece of paper and a pen or pencil.
- Have students list their own sins on the paper and then destroy it as a sign of the forgiveness.

TEAM EFFORT—HIGH SCHOOL (15-20 MINUTES)

THE BLOOD OF CHRIST
- Display a copy of the Blood of Christ" on page 177 using an overhead projector.
- As a whole group, complete the page.

Read Hebrews 9:11-22.

What is the significance of blood and forgiveness?

(Blood signifies that something has been sacrificed—taken the place for another—to bring about forgiveness.)

Why is the blood of Christ different from the blood of goats?

(Christ's blood is pure and without any blemish.)

What does verse 22 mean?

(It is only through the shedding of Christ's blood that we have forgiveness.)

Now read this incredible story.

A Gift Freely Given

Max Lucado is my favorite Christian author. He tells a story that I will never forget of a mother and her four-year-old daughter.

Susanna (the mom) and her daughter Gayaney were trying on clothes at her sister-in-law's home when the worst earthquake in the history of Armenia hit. There were fifty-five thousand victims in this one quake. They were on the fifth floor of an apartment building; the next thing they knew they had tumbled into the base-

---

Fold

---

ment. Susanna and Gayaney were still alive but they were totally stuck and could not get up. "Mommy, I need a drink. Please give me something," was the cry of little Gayaney. Susanna found a twenty-four ounce jar of blackberry jam that had fallen into the basement. She gave the entire jar to her daughter to eat. It was gone by the second day.

"Mommy, I'm thirsty." Susanna didn't know what to do.

Periodically Susanna would sleep but usually awakened from the whining and whimpering of her precious daughter. They were trapped for eight days. Susanna lost track of time. She was cold and numb, and she lost hope. "Mommy, I'm thirsty. Please give me something to drink." She then remembered that it was possible to drink blood! So she cut her left index finger and gave it to her daughter to suck. The drops of blood were not enough. "Please Mommy, some more. Cut another finger." Susanna had no idea how many times she cut herself but if she hadn't Gayaney would have died. Susanna's blood was her daughter's only hope.

Max Lucado writes about this episode this way:

"Beneath the rubble of a fallen world, he pierced his hands. In the wreckage of a collapsed humanity he ripped open his side. His children were trapped, so he gave freely his own blood.

It was all he had. His friends were gone. His strength was waning, his possessions had been gambled away at his feet. Even his father turned his head. His blood was all he had. But his blood was all it took.

If anyone is thirsty, Jesus once said, let him come to me and drink.

And the
hand
was pierced.

And the
blood
was poured.

And the
children
were saved."

IN THE WORD (25-30 MINUTES)

GOOD NEWS FOR THOSE WHO ARE IMPERFECT
- Ask several persons in your group to read John 8:1-11 sometime before the lesson and prepare a role play of this incredible drama. The only rules are that they have to act out the text as much as possible, and the woman caught in adultery must wear clothes!
- Students perform role play.
- Give each student a copy of "Good News for Those Who Are Imperfect" on pages 179 and 181 and a pen or pencil.
- Students complete the Bible study.

Read John 8:1-11.

1. If you were the woman how would you feel?

2. What do you think happened to the man who was caught but not brought to Jesus?

3. Why do you think Jesus drew in the dirt?

4. Why is the statement Jesus made in John 8:7 so powerful?

5. What points are important to remember from the conversation with Jesus and the woman in John 8:9-11?

 WARM UP

TRUE CONFESSIONS

My most embarrassing moment was:

....

....

Something very few people know about me is:

....

....

If I could go anywhere in the world I would go to:

....

....

If I could do or be anything it would be:

....

....

If I could choose to have a gift it would be:

....

....

....

175

TEAM EFFORT

THE BLOOD OF CHRIST

Read Hebrews 9:11-22.

What is the significance of blood and forgiveness?

....

Why is the blood of Christ different from the blood of goats?

....

What does verse 22 mean?

....

Now read this incredible story.

A Gift Freely Given

Max Lucado is my favorite Christian author. He tells a story that I will never forget of a mother and her four-year old daughter.

Susanna (the mom) and her daughter Gayaney were trying on clothes at her sister-in-law's home when the worst earthquake in the history of Armenia hit. There were fifty-five thousand victims in this one quake.

They were on the fifth floor of an apartment building; the next thing they knew they had tumbled into the basement. Susanna and Gayaney were still alive but they were totally stuck and could not get up. "Mommy, I need a drink. Please give me something," was the cry of little Gayaney. Susanna found a twenty-four ounce jar of blackberry jam that had fallen into the basement. She gave the entire jar to her daughter to eat. It was gone by the second day.

"Mommy, I'm thirsty." Susanna didn't know what to do. Truthfully, there was nothing she could do to help her daughter. They were trapped for eight days. Susanna lost track of time. She was cold and numb, and she lost hope. Periodically Susanna would sleep but usually awakened from the whining and whimpering of her precious daughter. "Mommy, I'm thirsty. Please give me something to drink." She then remembered that it was possible to drink blood! So she cut her left index finger and gave it to her daughter to suck. The drops of blood were not enough. "Please Mommy, some more. Cut another finger." Susanna had no idea how many times she cut herself but if she hadn't Gayaney would have died. Susanna's blood was her daughter's only hope.[1]

Max Lucado writes about this episode this way:

"Beneath the rubble of a fallen world, he pierced his hands. In the wreckage of a collapsed humanity he ripped open his side. His children were trapped, so he gave freely his own blood.

It was all he had. His friends were gone. His strength was waning, his possessions had been gambled away at his feet. Even his father turned his head. His blood was all he had. But his blood was all it took.

If anyone is thirsty, Jesus once said, let him come to me and drink.

And the	And the	And the
hand	blood	children
was pierced.	was poured.	were saved."[2]

Note

1. Jim Burns, *Spirit Wings* (Ann Arbor, MI: Vine Books, 1992), pp. 188-189.

2. Max Lucado, *The Applause of Heaven* (Dallas, TX: Word, Inc., 1990), p. 91.

IN THE WORD

GOOD NEWS FOR THOSE WHO ARE IMPERFECT

Read John 8:1-11

1. If you were the woman how would you feel?

2. What do you think happened to the man who was caught but not brought to Jesus?

3. Why do you think Jesus drew in the dirt?

4. Why is the statement Jesus made in John 8:7 so powerful?

5. What points are important to remember from the conversation with Jesus and the woman in John 8:9-11?

The word "confess" actually means to agree. Confessing your sins to God is agreeing with God that you, like everyone else, fall short of perfection.

Read these verses on confession and forgiveness and discuss what they mean.

1 John 1:9

Psalm 86:5

Isaiah 1:18

Hebrews 10:17

**CONFESSION AND
FORGIVENESS**

So what?

For I will forgive their wickedness and will remember their sins no more
(Jeremiah 31:34).

According to this verse what will Christ do with your confessed sins?

....

....

....

What keeps you from taking a few moments right now and confessing your sins to the Lord?

....

....

....

Things to Think About

1. Why is it easier to accept God's forgiveness than forgive ourselves?

....

....

....

2. What makes confession to another person such a powerful experience? (See James 5:16.)

....

....

....

3. Where does the idea of repentance come into the picture of forgiveness?

....

....

....

PARENT PAGE

A COMMON RESPONSE

Saint Peter's Square, May 1981, was the scene of a terrible event that shocked the world: an assassination attempt on Pope John Paul II.

The scene was quite different nearly three years later when Pope John Paul sat in Rome's Rebibbia Prison holding the hand of his would-be assassin, Mehment Ali Agca. The Pope forgave the man for the shooting. What a tremendous story of forgiveness and reconciliation. While the Pope whispered quietly in the cell, he preached a message loud and clear to the entire world. He communicated the message of Christ.

1. How would you feel about a man who attempted to kill you?

....

....

2. What do you think the assassin was feeling after the Pope's message of forgiveness?

....

....

3. How can you proclaim the same message of Christ in your world and family today?

....

....

4. Unfortunately, it is uncommon in our world to forgive and forget. Most people do not cancel debts, especially large ones. But Jesus does. Why is confession and repentance an important process of our faith in Christ?

....

....

5. Read Matthew 6:14,15. How does God's forgiveness for you affect the way you treat others?

....

....

6. Do you need to cancel a debt by extending forgiveness to someone who has wronged you, whether he or she is in the family or outside the family?

....

....

Session 10 "Confession and Forgiveness" Date ....

THANKSGIVING

KEY VERSE

"**G**ive thanks in all circumstances, for this is God's will for you in Christ Jesus." 1 Thessalonians 5:18

BIBLICAL BASIS

Psalm 7:17; 50:4; 92:1-4; 100:1-5; 107:1; 136:1; 138:1; **R**omans 5:8; **1** Thessalonians 5:18

THE BIG IDEA

Creating an attitude of thankfulness is definitely a life-changing experience. Thankful people are happy people.

AIMS OF THIS SESSION

During this session you will guide students to:

• Examine how thankfulness can transform a negative attitude into a positive one;

• Discover from the Scripture the spiritual principles and power of thankfulness;

• Implement a practice of thanksgiving in their lives.

WARM UP

Thankful Brainstorm—
A list of reasons to be thankful.

TEAM EFFORT— JUNIOR HIGH/ MIDDLE SCHOOL

Banners of Thanks—
Students create banners of thanks.

TEAM EFFORT— HIGH SCHOOL

A Modern-Day Psalm—
Students write their own psalm of thanksgiving.

IN THE WORD

Thankfulness—
A Bible study on developing and living out an attitude of thanksgiving.

THINGS TO THINK ABOUT (OPTIONAL)

Questions to get students thinking and talking about being thankful.

PARENT PAGE

A tool to get the session into the home and allow parents and young people to show thanks for each other.

LEADER'S DEVOTIONAL

Most of us have struggled at one time or another with knowing God's will in the big issues—where He wants us to move or which job He wants us to take. But even for those of us who have never had a big decision to bring to God, we can solidly know His will! For Paul tells us in 1 Thessalonians 5:18 that it is God's will for us to give thanks in all circumstances! *All* circumstances! That's a pretty broad variety of places from which to start understanding God's will!

Now how does being thankful in every weird, irritating circumstance relate to the will of the almighty Creator of the universe? Does this mean being thankful when we are pulled over by a patrolman instead of ranting to ourselves as we drive away with a ticket? That's hard to swallow!

But that's precisely it. Because the thing that's most difficult to swallow is our pride. Pride is the root of all other sins, the spawning ground for every kind of rebellion that makes our lives miserable and our hearts resistant to the gentle moving of God's Spirit. And when we find ourselves in what we see as trouble, we have two choices: we have to drop our pride and let go of our own way, or grab for control even more desperately. As James 4:10 says, "Humble yourselves before the Lord, and he will lift you up."

When we give thanks to God in any situation, we acknowledge both to God and to ourselves just who we are—little people who need Him—and who He is, the only One who can help us. We are humbled and ready to hear what He has to say to us. That's not only God's will *for* us to be thankful, it's also the place in our hearts to which we must come to begin to see His will in other ways.

God is looking for people who *are* something inside, first and foremost, before they are people who *do* something. Be thankful! It's the attitude of the open heart. (Mary Gross, editor, Gospel Light.)

"The prayer of thanksgiving should be quite specific....If we are 'thankful for everything,' we may end by being thankful for nothing."—

George Arthur Buttrick, *Prayer* (Abingdon-Cokesbury, 1942)

THANKSGIVING

KEY VERSE

"Give thanks in all circumstances, for this is God's will for you in Christ Jesus."
1 Thessalonians 5:18

BIBLICAL BASIS

Psalm 7:17; 50:4; 92:1-4; 100:1-5; 107:1; 136:1; 138:1; Romans 5:8; 1 Thessalonians 5:18

THE BIG IDEA

Creating an attitude of thankfulness is definitely a life-changing experience. Thankful people are happy people.

WARM UP (5-10 MINUTES)

THANKFUL BRAINSTORM

- Divide students into groups of three or four.
- Give each group a sheet of newsprint and a felt pen.
- Students brainstorm and list several horrible situations in our nation (i.e., hunger, homelessness, divorce, etc.). Then brainstorm and list reasons why a person could be thankful in the midst of these devastating situations.
- As a whole group, students share their ideas.

TEAM EFFORT—JUNIOR HIGH/MIDDLE SCHOOL (15-20 MINUTES)

BANNERS OF THANKS

- Divide students into groups of three or four.
- Give each group a piece of newsprint and felt pens.
- Read aloud Psalm 34:1-4; 92:1-4.
- Students create a banner expressing thanks to God.
- As a whole group, students share their banners.

---

3. Why do you think Christmas and Easter are special times of thanksgiving for Christians?

4. How do you think it makes God feel when we are thankful?

5. How do you think it makes God feel when we complain?

PARENT PAGE

- Distribute page to parents.

TEAM EFFORT—HIGH SCHOOL (15–20 MINUTES)

A MODERN-DAY PSALM

- Divide students into groups of three or four.
- Assign each group one of the following verses: Psalm 7:17; Psalm 34:1-4; Psalm 50:4; Psalm 92:1-4; Psalm 100:1-5; Psalm 107:1; Psalm 136:1; Psalm 138:1.
- Give each group a piece of paper and a pen or pencil.
- Have students write their own modern-day thanksgiving psalm.
- As a whole group, students share their psalms.

IN THE WORD (25–30 MINUTES)

THANKFULNESS

- Divide students into groups of three or four.
- Give each student a copy of "Thankfulness" on pages 189 and 191 and a pen or pencil.
- Students complete the Bible study.

Over and over again the Scripture tells us to be thankful people. No one can read the psalms (songs of the Hebrew people) and not be affected by the theme of thankfulness running through the pages of that great hymnal. As you look around, think for a moment: Who are the happy and fulfilled people you know? Most likely these people are also thankful and grateful people.

Where do you fit in on the thankfulness scale? Are you a grumbler and complainer, or do you consider yourself a thankful and grateful person? Mark an *X* where you fit on this scale.

Grumbler/Complainer   Grateful/Thankful Person

Christians have much to be thankful for. Yet we all struggle at times with being ungrateful servants in our Father's house. Here are three points to help us to be more thankful people.

1. Thankfulness is an attitude.

a. In 1 Thessalonians 5:18 Paul tells us what God's will is for our lives. Read 1 Thessalonians 5:18. When I read that I should be thankful in all situations, I:

.... 1. believe it, but it is hard to put into practice.

.... 2. think it is impossible to do.

.... 3. don't understand exactly what Paul is trying to say in this verse.

.... 4. wish I could develop that trait in my life.

Notice that the Scripture does not say to be thankful *for* all situations. It says to be thankful in all situations. How ridiculous to be thankful for a negative problem! But when we are challenged to be thankful in all circumstances, it is much easier to see that even in difficult times there are reasons to be thankful.

b. What's a difficult situation that you are experiencing right now? What's one thing that you can be thankful for in that situation?

....

--- Fold ---

2. Make thankfulness a habit in your life.

We all have good habits and bad habits. Often we focus on our bad habits; yet as Christians we need to work on developing good habits. If you develop the good habit of placing thankfulness in your heart on a daily basis, your life will be better in every way.

Thank Therapy puts into practice Paul's command to be thankful in all situations. Thank Therapy is writing on paper 20 reasons why you are thankful. At first glance 20 reasons looks like a lot, but as you begin writing you'll find that you can list these 20 reasons. You'll see how helpful it is to be reminded of God's blessings in your life. As you become consciously aware of why you are thankful to God for what He has already done for you, great things will begin to develop in your spirit. Let's practice Thank Therapy!

List 20 things for which you are thankful (i.e., Jesus Christ, family, your church, eyeglasses, health, weather, etc.). Now take a few minutes to share a few with your group.

1. ....   11. ....
2. ....   12. ....
3. ....   13. ....
4. ....   14. ....
5. ....   15. ....
6. ....   16. ....
7. ....   17. ....
8. ....   18. ....
9. ....   19. ....
10. ....   20. ....

3. Jesus Christ paid the ultimate sacrifice for our sin, because of this we can be thankful.

a. What is the good news found in Romans 5:8?

....

b. How can this point help you be thankful even when things are getting difficult?

....

SO WHAT?

How will you take the principles of thankfulness and use them in your life this week?

....

THINGS TO THINK ABOUT (OPTIONAL)

- Use the questions on page 193 after or as a part of "In the Word."

1. Why do we tend to focus on the negative instead of the positive?

....

2. List several reasons why thankful people are usually happier people.

....

IN THE WORD

THANKFULNESS

Over and over again the Scripture tells us to be thankful people. No one can read the psalms (songs of the Hebrew people) and not be affected by the theme of thankfulness running through the pages of that great hymnal. As you look around, think for a moment: Who are the happy and fulfilled people you know? Most likely these people are also thankful and grateful people.

Where do you fit in on the thankfulness scale? Are you a grumbler and complainer, or do you consider yourself a thankful and grateful person? Mark an *X* where you fit on this scale.

Grumbler/Complainer   Grateful/Thankful Person

Christians have much to be thankful for. Yet we all struggle at times with being ungrateful servants in our Father's house. Here are three points to help us to be more thankful people.

1. Thankfulness is an attitude.

   a. In 1 Thessalonians 5:18 Paul tells us what God's will is for our lives. Read
   1 Thessalonians 5:18. When I read that I should be thankful in all situations, I:

       .... **1. believe it, but it is hard to put into practice.**

       .... **2. think it is impossible to do.**

       .... **3. don't understand exactly what Paul is trying to say in this verse.**

       .... **4. wish I could develop that trait in my life.**

Notice that the Scripture does not say to be thankful *for* all situations. It says to be thankful *in* all situations. How ridiculous to be thankful for a negative problem! But when we are challenged to be thankful in all circumstances, it is much easier to see that even in difficult times there are reasons to be thankful.

   b. What's a difficult situation that you are experiencing right now? What's one thing that you can be thankful for in that situation?

....

....

2. Make thankfulness a habit in your life.

We all have good habits and bad habits. Often we focus on our bad habits; yet as Christians we need to work on developing good habits. If you develop the good habit of placing thankfulness in your heart on a daily basis, your life will be better in every way.

Thank Therapy puts into practice Paul's command to "be thankful in all situations." Thank therapy is writing on paper 20 reasons why you are thankful. At first glance 20 reasons looks like a lot, but as you begin writing you'll find that you can list these 20 reasons. You'll see how helpful it is to be reminded of God's blessings in your life. As you become

consciously aware of why you are thankful to God for what He has already done for you, great things will begin to develop in your spirit. Let's practice Thank Therapy!

List 20 things for which you are thankful (i.e., Jesus Christ, family, your church, eyeglasses, health, weather, etc.). Now take a few minutes to share a few with your group.

1. ....
2. ....
3. ....
4. ....
5. ....
6. ....
7. ....
8. ....
9. ....
10. ....

11. ....
12. ....
13. ....
14. ....
15. ....
16. ....
17. ....
18. ....
19. ....
20. ....

3. Jesus Christ paid the ultimate sacrifice for our sin; because of this we can be thankful.

a. What is the good news found in Romans 5:8?

....

....

....

b. How can this point help you be thankful even when things are getting difficult?

....

....

....

So WHAT?

How will you take the principles of thankfulness and use them in your life this week?

....

....

....

....

Things to Think About

1. Why do we tend to focus on the negative instead of the positive?

....

....

....

2. List several reasons why thankful people are usually happier people.

....

....

....

3. Why do you think Christmas and Easter are special times of thanksgiving for Christians?

....

....

....

4. How do you think it makes God feel when we are thankful?

....

....

....

5. How do you think it makes God feel when we complain?

....

....

....

PARENT PAGE

Give thanks in all circumstances, for this is God's will for you in Christ Jesus
(1 Thessalonians 5:18).

1. What important truths do you find in this Scripture?

....

....

....

2. How can we practice thankfulness in our home more often?

....

....

....

3. What is the significance of these quotes. Read and discuss them.

"I complained because I had no shoes until I met a man who had no feet."—Old Indian Proverb

"Thankfulness transcends your circumstances. Your circumstances may never change, but your attitude can change and that makes all the difference in the world."—Jim Burns

The Thanks Bombardment Game

Each family member completes this sentence for every other family member.

I am thankful to God for (family member's name) because:

Session 11 "Thanksgiving" Date ....

ASKING

Key Verses

"Then he said to them, 'Suppose one of you has a friend, and he goes to him at midnight and says, "Friend, lend me three loaves of bread, because a friend of mine on a journey has come to me, and I have nothing to set before him,'

'Then the one inside answers, "Don't bother me. The door is already locked, and my children are with me in bed. I can't get up and give you anything." I tell you, though he will not get up and give him the bread because he is his friend, yet because of the man's boldness he will get up and give him as much as he needs.

'So I say to you: Ask and it will be given to you; seek and you will find; knock and the door will be opened to you. For everyone who asks receives; he who seeks finds; and to him who knocks, the door will be opened.

'Which of you fathers, if your son asks for a fish, will give him snake instead? Or if he asks for an egg, will give him a scorpion? If you then, though you are evil, know how to give good gifts to your children, how much more will your Father in heaven give the Holy Spirit to those who ask him!'" Luke 11:5-13

Biblical Basis

Matthew 7:7-12; 21:22;
Luke 11:5-13;
Hebrews 11:1;
1 John 5:14,15

The Big Idea

God is a loving Lord who hears the persistent prayers of His children.

Aims of This Session

During this session you will guide students to:

- Examine the principles of asking in their prayer lives;
- Discover that God loves them and wants to hear their prayers of asking;
- Implement an attitude of submission to God's will as they ask Him to do His work in their lives.

Warm Up

Prayer Is—
Students share their views on prayer.

Team Effort— Junior High/ Middle School

Ask, Seek, Receive—
A letter asking God to meet specific needs.

Team Effort— High School

A Concert of Prayer—
A time of intercessory prayer.

In The Word

The Friend at Midnight—
A Bible study on persistently asking of God.

Things To Think About (OPTIONAL)

Questions to get students thinking and talking about prayer.

Parent Page

A tool to get the session into the home and allow parents and young people to develop a family prayer journal.

Leader's Devotional

Perhaps at the beginning of this study, some of us thought asking was the main purpose of prayer. But hopefully, as we've studied and lived out what we've learned so far, it's become clear that prayer is really far more than getting together with God to tick off lists of our needs and desires.

Certainly asking is only part of the larger picture of intimate relationship with God. But it is a viable and vital part of our talking with and listening to our Father. Jesus made it clear to us that we should ask God for everything we need, from our simplest daily needs like food to the thousands of dollars needed to fund a missions project.

In studying men and women for whom prayer was an integral part of their lives, we find that they never hesitated to ask God for the smallest (and what we might consider the silliest) things. If a shilling was needed to make up a payment, they prayed. If a pen was lost, they asked God to help them find it. But isn't this far too trivial for God?

Again, it's a part of the growing fabric of prayer that covers our lives as we live in closer intimacy with Him. Just as we find that our hunger for God increases as we feed on His Word more, so also we find that as we talk with Him more, we want to talk more with Him! We begin to discover that in the context of that daily closeness, it's really OK to ask Him for the smallest help, to invite His direction in the smallest detail! As Jesus said, if we know how to give good gifts to our own children, how much more loving, how much more desirous to help us, is our infinitely loving Father! He wants to hear from each of us. Our Perfect Father waits for us to come and be held close while we whisper our needs into His ear, perfectly free in our hearts that He will take perfect care of us! He delights to have His children tell Him what they need, nestling in trust against Him and secure in the knowledge that He will do everything for us! (Mary Gross, editor, Gospel Light.)

"God needs, greatly needs, priests who can draw near to Him, who live in His presence, and by their intercession draw down the blessings of His grace on others.—

Andrew Murray, *With Christ in the School of Prayer* (Revell, 1953)

BIBLE TUCK-IN™

ASKING

KEY VERSES

"Then he said to them, 'Suppose one of you has a friend, and he goes to him at midnight and says, "Friend, lend me three loaves of bread, because a friend of mine on a journey has come to me, and I have nothing to set before him."

"Then the one inside answers, 'Don't bother me. The door is already locked, and my children are with me in bed. I can't get up and give you anything.' I tell you, though he will not get up and give him the bread because he is his friend, yet because of the man's boldness he will get up and give him as much as he needs.

"So I say to you: Ask and it will be given to you; seek and you will find; knock and the door will be opened to you. For everyone who asks receives; he who seeks finds; and to him who knocks, the door will be opened.

"Which of you fathers, if your son asks for a fish, will give him snake instead? Or if he asks for an egg, will give him a scorpion? If you then, though you are evil, know how to give good gifts to your children, how much more will your Father in heaven give the Holy Spirit to those who ask him!'" Luke 11:5-13

BIBLICAL BASIS

Matthew 7:7-12; 21:22; Luke 11:5-13; Hebrews 11:1; 1 John 5:14,15

THE BIG IDEA

God is a loving Lord who hears the persistent prayers of His children.

WARM UP (5-10 MINUTES)

PRAYER IS

• Display a copy of "Prayer Is" on page 201 using an overhead projector.
• Divide students into groups of three or four.
• Students complete statements.

Prayer is not:

Prayer is:

The best place for me to pray is:

The worst place for me to pray is:

The hardest thing about prayer is:

The greatest thing about prayer is:

Fold

Prayer was instrumental in the rise of Israel in Old Testament times. God chose to use the prayer of Hannah, a humble woman, to help bring about Israel's greatness.

1. Read Hannah's prayer found in 1 Samuel 1:10,11. What are some of the features of her prayer?

2. What gift did Hannah receive from the Lord? (See 1 Samuel 1:20.)

Samuel grew to be a great prophet and leader of Israel. It was Samuel who anointed David when God chose David to be king of Israel.

SO WHAT?

How do the following verses influence your attitude about prayer?

Matthew 21:22

Hebrews 11:1

1 John 5:14,15

According to these verses what specifically are you asking God to accomplish in your life?

THINGS TO THINK ABOUT (OPTIONAL)

• Use the questions on page 211 after or as a part of "In the Word."

1. If prayer is so effective, why do Christians pray so little?

2. What has been the biggest help to your prayer life?

3. What is the greatest need you have and want to give to God in prayer?

PARENT PAGE

• Distribute page to parents.

TEAM EFFORT—JUNIOR HIGH/MIDDLE SCHOOL (15-20 MINUTES)

ASK, SEEK, RECEIVE

- Give each student a copy of "Ask, Seek, Receive" on page 203, a pen or pencil and an envelope.
- Students individually write a letter asking God to meet specific needs.
- Have students seal letters in envelopes and address them to themselves. Then mail their letters to them three months later.

A Letter to God

Ask and it will be given to you; seek and you will find; knock and the door will be opened to you. For everyone who asks receives; he who seeks finds; and to him who knocks, the door will be opened.

Which of you, if his son asks for bread, will give him a stone? Or if he asks for a fish, will give him a snake? If you, then, though you are evil, know how to give good gifts to your children, how much more will your Father in heaven give good gifts to those who ask him! So in everything, do to others what you would have them do to you, for this sums up the Law and the Prophets (Matthew 7:7-12).

TEAM EFFORT—HIGH SCHOOL (15-20 MINUTES)

A CONCERT OF PRAYER

- Display a copy of "A Concert of Prayer" on page 205 using an overhead projector.
- Divide students into groups of three or four.
- Students pray for needs listed.

Pray for the needs of our community, school, job.
Pray for the needs of our church.
Pray for the needs of missions, the "10/40 Window" (the people in the area of the world from 10 degrees to 40 degrees north latitude).
Pray for our president and government leadership.
Pray for the personal purity and lifestyle of our church leaders. (Don't forget to thank God for them.)
Pray for your family (specifically and by name).
Pray for your own life.
Listen to the names the Spirit places on your mind and pray for them.

IN THE WORD (25-30 MINUTES)

THE FRIEND AT MIDNIGHT

- Divide students into pairs.
- Give each student a copy of "The Friend at Midnight" on page 207 and a pen or pencil.
- Have students perform role play.
- Students complete the Bible study.

Then he said to them, "Suppose one of you has a friend, and he goes to him at midnight and says, 'Friend, lend me three loaves of bread, because a friend of mine on a journey has come to me, and I have nothing to set before him.'

"Then the one inside answers, 'Don't bother me. The door is already locked, and my children are with me in bed. I can't get up and give you anything.' I tell you, though he will not get up and give him the bread because he is his friend, yet because of the man's boldness he will get up and give him as much as he needs.

"So I say to you: Ask and it will be given to you; seek and you will find; knock and the door will be opened to you. For everyone who asks receives; he who seeks finds; and to him who knocks, the door will be opened" (Luke 11:5-10).

Go back 2000 years to Israel. You are sleeping in your home with your spouse and children. There is a knock on the door, though it's past midnight. You don't want to wake up the kids. You hope whoever it is will go away. But they don't. They keep knocking. Finally, you get up. You find your neighbor who tells you that he has unexpected guests, and he needs to borrow some food from you. (The convenience store in Jerusalem is already closed!) Now act out the story in any way you want. You can modernize the story if you wish.

Read Luke 11:5-13.

Answer these questions.

1. What characteristics of the friend at the door caused the person to finally open up the door?

2. What was the point to Jesus' story?

3. What kind of invitation do we receive in Luke 11:9,10?

4. What do you think keeps most believers from asking, seeking and knocking more often?

5. It is important to note that the Greek words ask, knock, seek are all written in the present tense, which is best translated: keep on asking, keep on knocking and keep on seeking. How does this knowledge help your understanding of verses 9 and 10?

The Good Gifts of the Father
Read Luke 11:11-13.

1. Why do you think Jesus compared the gifts of a good earthly father with the response of our heavenly Father?

Fold

WARM UP

PRAYER IS

Prayer is not:...

....

Prayer is:...

....

The best place for me to pray is:...

....

The worst place for me to pray is:...

....

The hardest thing about prayer is:..

....

The greatest thing about prayer is:...

....

TEAM EFFORT

ASK, SEEK, RECEIVE

Ask and it will be given to you; seek and you will find; knock and the door will be opened to you. For everyone who asks receives; he who seeks finds; and to him who knocks, the door will be opened.

Which of you, if his son asks for bread, will give him a stone? Or if he asks for a fish, will give him a snake? If you, then, though you are evil, know how to give good gifts to your children, how much more will your Father in heaven give good gifts to those who ask him! So in everything, do to others what you would have them do to you, for this sums up the Law and the Prophets (Matthew 7: 7-12).

A Letter to God

....

....

....

....

....

....

....

....

....

....

....

....

....

....

....

....

....

....

....

203

A CONCERT OF PRAYER
Pray for the needs of our community, school, job.

Pray for the needs of our church.

Pray for the needs of missions, the "10/40 Window" (the people in the area of the world from 10 degrees to 40 degrees north latitude).

Pray for our president and government leadership.

Pray for the personal purity and lifestyle of our church leaders. (Don't forget to thank God for them.)

Pray for your family (specifically and by name).

Pray for your own life.

Listen to the names the Spirit places on your mind and pray for them.

THE FRIEND AT MIDNIGHT

> Then he said to them, "Suppose one of you has a friend, and he goes to him at midnight and says, 'Friend, lend me three loaves of bread, because a friend of mine on a journey has come to me, and I have nothing to set before him.'
>
> "Then the one inside answers, 'Don't bother me. The door is already locked, and my children are with me in bed. I can't get up and give you anything.' I tell you, though he will not get up and give him the bread because he is his friend, yet because of the man's boldness he will get up and give him as much as he needs.
>
> "So I say to you: Ask and it will be given to you; seek and you will find; knock and the door will be opened to you. For everyone who asks receives; he who seeks finds; and to him who knocks, the door will be opened" (Luke 11:5-10).

Go back 2000 years to Israel. You are sleeping in your home with your spouse and children. There is a knock on the door, though it's past midnight. You don't want to wake up the kids. You hope whoever it is will go away. But they don't. They keep knocking. Finally, you get up. You find your neighbor who tells you that he has unexpected guests, and he needs to borrow some food from you. (The convenience store in Jerusalem is already closed!) Now act out the story in any way you want. You can modernize the story if you wish.

After the role play, read Luke 11:5-13.

Answer these questions.

1. What characteristics of the friend at the door caused the person to finally open up the door?

....

....

2. What was the point to Jesus' story?

....

....

3. What kind of invitation do we receive in Luke 11:9,10?

....

....

207

4. What do you think keeps most believers from asking, seeking and knocking more often?

....

....

5. It is important to note that the Greek words *ask, knock* and *seek* are all written in the present tense, which is best translated: keep on asking, keep on knocking and keep on seeking. How does this knowledge help your understanding of
verses 9 and 10?

....

....

The Good Gifts of the Father
Read Luke 11:11-13.
1. Why do you think Jesus compared the gifts of a good earthly father with the response of our heavenly Father?

....

....

Prayer was instrumental in the rise of Israel in Old Testament times. God chose to use the prayer
of Hannah, a humble woman, to help bring about Israel's greatness.

1. Read Hannah's prayer found in 1 Samuel 1:10,11. What are some of the features of her prayer?

....

....

2. What gift did Hannah receive from the Lord? (See 1 Samuel 1:20.)

....

....

Samuel grew to be a great prophet and leader of Israel. It was Samuel who anointed David when
God chose David to be king of Israel.

So What?

How do the following verses influence your attitude about prayer?

Matthew 21:22

Hebrews 11:1

1 John 5:14,15

According to these verses what specifically are you asking God to accomplish in your life?

Things to Think About

1. If prayer is so effective, why do Christians pray so little?

2. What has been the biggest help to your prayer life?

3. What is the greatest need you have and want to give to God in prayer?

PARENT PAGE

FAMILY PRAYER JOURNAL

Create a prayer list for your family. Ask for prayer requests; write them on a large piece of paper and then as a family take several minutes to pray for each request. Each week check in on each request.

....

....

....

....

....

....

....

....

....

....

....

....

....

....

....

....

....

....

Session 12 "Asking" Date ....

Add a New Member to Your Youth Staff.

Jim Burns is president of the
National Institute of Youth Ministry.

Meet Jim Burns. He won't play guitar and he doesn't do windows, but he will take care of your programming needs. That's because his new curriculum, **YouthBuilders Group Bible Studies** is a comprehensive program designed to take your group through their high school years. (If you have jr. high kids in your group, **YouthBuilders** works for them too.)

For less than $6 a month you'll get Jim Burns' special recipe of high-involvement, discussion-oriented, Bible-centered studies. It's the next generation of Bible curriculum for youth—and with Jim on your staff, you'll be free to spend more time one-on-one with the kids in your group.

Volume 1 of the YouthBuilders curriculum series is:
The Word on Sex, Drugs & Rock 'N' Roll
ISBN #08307.16424
**Look for these issues in other
volumes of Youthbuilders–**
- Prayer, Developing a Devotional Life
- Next Step for New Believers, Christian Basics
- Peer Leadership, Spiritual Gifts and Sharing Your Faith
- Servanthood, Commitment, Discipleship
- Crisis Issues and Peer Counseling

Here are some of YouthBuilders hottest features

- **Reproducible pages–**
  one book fits your whole group
- **Wide appeal–**
  big groups, small groups–even adjusts to fit jr. high/high school groups
- **Hits home–**
  special section to involve parents with every session of the study
- **Interactive Bible discovery–**
  geared to help young people find answers themselves
- **Cheat sheets–**
  a Bible *Tuck-In*™ with all the session information on a single page
- **Flexible format–**
  perfect for Sunday mornings, midweek youth meetings, or camps and retreats
- **Three studies in one–**
  each study has three, four-session modules examining critical life choices.

A Push-Button Course for Junior High.

Jr. High Builders are all-in-one programs that help kids put their faith in action. Each book in the series includes 13 Bible studies, dozens of games and activities as well as clip art to illustrate your handouts—all you have to do is warm up the copier!

Jr. High Builders titles include:
- Christian Basics (ISBN 08307.16963)
- Christian Relationships (ISBN 08307.16491)
- Symbols of Christ (ISBN 08307.15126)
- Power of God (ISBN08307.17048)
- Faith in Action (ISBN 08307.17056)
- Life-Styles of the Not-so-Famous from the Bible
  (ISBN 08307.17099)
and many others - 12 in all!

Gospel Light

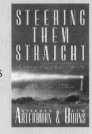
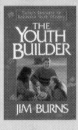